LONDON
An Illustrated History

Robert Chester & Nicholas Awde

Additional photographs & illustrations
by Nicholas Awde

HIPPOCRENE BOOKS, INC.
NEW YORK

ACKNOWLEDGMENTS

Thea Khitarishvili, Fiona Robertson, Andrew Honey, Ian "Knox" Carnochan, Emanuela Losi, Anne Kemper, Ken Livingstone, Heal's, Selfridge's, Greater London Authority, British Museum, British Library, Imperial War Museum, Elstree Film & Television Studios, Peabody Trust, Canary Wharf Group, Cameron Mackintosh Productions, B.B.C., Royal Courts of Justice, Transport for London, The History of Advertising Trust, Fosters & Partners.

ILLUSTRATION CREDITS

Additional photographs, drawings & maps by Nicholas Awde.
Thanks to Ian M. Carnochan for extra illustrations.
Where possible, every effort has been made to trace copyright holders of illustrations that appear in this book. Any unwitting infringement will be rectified in future editions.

Image on first page: Liberty department store, designed by Edwin T. Hall and his son Edwin S. Hallat at the height of the 1920s fashion for Tudor revival and built from the timbers of two ships: HMS Impregnable and HMS Hindustan. The frontage of the Great Marlborough Street store is the same length as the Hindustan.

Typeset & designed by Nick Awde/Desert♥Hearts

ISBN 0-7818-0908-8

For information, address:
HIPPOCRENE BOOKS, INC.
171 Madison Avenue
New York, NY 10016
www.hippocrenebooks.com

Printed in the United States of America.

CONTENTS

LONDON
IS ONE OF THE FINEST CITIES IN THE WORLD . . .

It's a boast that I make not just because I am a Londoner born and bred, nor because I am the city's first directly-elected mayor in its history. Quite simply, London's economic strength, its size and diversity, and its cultural range combine to make it one of the few genuinely "world" cities anywhere.

London has always been at the center of world commerce and alongside New York it remains a powerful center of the global financial sector. Once home to one of the world's largest docks it now acts as a powerhouse for global business. And the capital can also claim to be the engine without which the rest of Britain would flounder. Its contribution to a vibrant national economy is therefore vital.

The city's importance has meant that its buildings and architecture are world famous: from the 900-year-old walls of the Tower of London to the dizzy heights of

Canary Wharf, the solid and tangible face of London is indelibly etched into the minds of millions of tourists who each year visit the capital.

Equally, the impact of the city on world culture has been enormous. From Shakespeare's first performances of his plays in Southwark and Georg Friedrich Handel's 47 years in London, which so inspired much of his finest music, to the contribution young Londoners are making now to popular music internationally, London remains a cultural dynamo.

Today London is famous for its ethnic and cultural diversity. More than 300 languages are regularly spoken among the city's seven million people. London's diversity—which is one of the features of the great world cities—helps make our capital such an attractive place for international business to invest.

Like all major cities, London has its problems: while London contains some of the greatest wealth in the world, it also has to cope with some of the worst social deprivation in Britain. Making cities a better place to live is one of the biggest challenges facing our society.

I am certainly very privileged to have been elected to serve such a wonderful place and I am sure that this book will add to the pride that those who live there, work there and visit the city feel towards it.

—by Ken Livingstone
The capital's first ever Mayor of London

"When a man is tired of London he is tired of life; for there is in London all that life can afford."
—Samuel Johnson

London Today

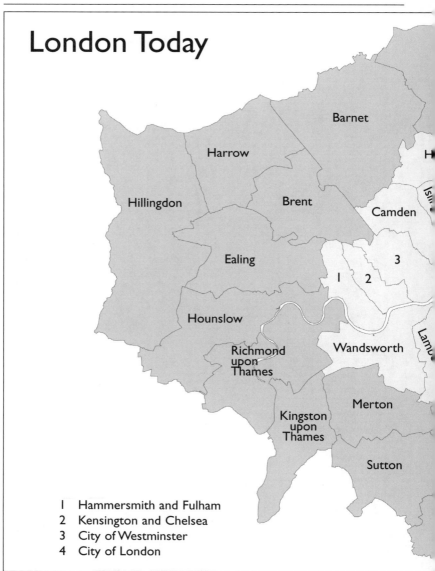

1 Hammersmith and Fulham
2 Kensington and Chelsea
3 City of Westminster
4 City of London

Enfield

ey

Waltham
Forest

Redbridge

Havering

Haringey

Tower
Hamlets

Newham

Barking &
Dagenham

Southwark

Greenwich

Bexley

Lewisham

Bromley

Croydon

Inner London
Boroughs

Outer London
Boroughs

CHAPTER 1
CITY ON THE THAMES

"For first, the City of London is built upon a sweet and most agreeable Eminency of Ground, at the North-side of a goodly and well-conditioned River, towards which it hath an Aspect by a gentle and easie declivity, apt to be improved to all that may render her Palaces, Buildings, and Avenues usefull, gracefull, and most magnificent: The Fumes which exhale from the Waters and lower Grounds lying Southward, by which means they are perpetually attracted, carried off, or dissipated by the Sun, as soon as they are born, and ascend."
—John Evelyn, *Fumifugium* (1661)

MODERN LONDON, THE BIGGEST and richest city in the United Kingdom, is a vast sprawling metropolis that stretches some 30 miles from east to west and 28 miles from south to north, with a population of over seven and a quarter million people. Greater London, as this area is known, is composed of 32 London boroughs and countless towns and villages all clustered around the ancient city area. Of such importance to the nation is this one city that much of the history of London *is* the history of England.

But despite this, at its very heart lies a small nucleus: the City of London, sometimes called "The Square Mile" or just "The City." This is the oldest part, the original city of Londinium founded by the Romans in the first century A.D. and originally enclosed by the ancient city walls. Today, just as it has always been, the City is a major mercantile and financial center.

To the west of the City, and connected to it by the Strand, lies the second city of the metropolis: the City of Westminster, sometimes called the "West End." This is the heart of Royal London.

Above left: A statue of King Charles I stands before his hunting lodge in Soho Square.
Above: Visitors at the Greenwich Meridian at the Greenwich Observatory.

The River Thames and Central London

Ker

Kew Gardens

Richmond Park

In the great Westminster Abbey church of this city, the monarch is crowned and Parliament meets in the Palace of Westminster, while Whitehall, next door, is the home of the various departments and ministries of government and is also on the site of an ancient royal palace. Yet Westminster is not just a city of royal history—the monarch's official residence of Buckingham Palace is here, and so too is the Palace of St. James, home to the royal court.

Legislation in the 19th century ruled that no railway lines could cross the city center, so a ring of termini were constructed around it. St. Pancras (below) is on of the finest examples of the way these were made into "cathedrals for travelers."

To the south of these two cities and separated from them by the River Thames lies an area called simply the "Borough." Now part of the London Borough of Southwark, this was the first town to grow up in London's shadow, beginning as a small settlement clustered round the southern end of London Bridge and the Old Kent Road, a route first built by the Romans to the channel ports. For many centuries, the Borough catered to the seedier aspects of London life since it was here that many brothels were located safe beyond the reach of the city authorities on the north banks of the river.

The final element at the heart of London

1. Westminster Abbey
2. Houses of Parliament & Whitehall
3. Trafalgar Square
4. St. Paul's Cathedral
5. Southwark Cathedral
6. London Bridge
7. Tower of London
8. Tower Bridge
9. Thames Flood Barrier

lies directly to the east of the City: the "East End," which was the industrial and manufacturing center of London. Being outside the ancient city walls, the East End was never subject to the various guilds that governed the City itself, and here artisans and craftsmen could set up shop without restriction. In turn the East End became home to factories and industry, and it was here that the first London Docks were opened in the early 19th century. The availability of work meant the East End became a magnet for some of the first immigrants to London, and the area has been home to, among others, French Huguenot, Irish, Italian, Jewish, Asian, and African communities.

City of contrasts: the Greater London Authority's City Hall (above), cloisters (below left) in the ancient Inns of Court's Inner Temple, and High Holborn (below right).

Currents of time

Around this heart, the modern metropolitan city has grown. But there is not just one London, there are many. Each Londoner and visitor has his or her own London, their own favorite elements that make up this vast, cosmopolitan and historic city. But to understand the rise of London one must first understand how it was shaped by the great tidal River Thames and the tributaries that run through its heart.

At the time of the Roman invasion in A.D. 43, the Thames would have been a wide meandering waterway about half a mile wide (1,000 meters) at high tide. While its northern bank was clearly defined by high ground, it was bounded on the southern side by wide marshes and mud flats that were exposed at low tide. The first fordable point of the river was probably upstream at Westminster, but just a little way downstream the geography of the land allowed a more permanent crossing point to be established. In the vicinity of modern Southwark, two gravel islands jutted out into the fast flowing center of the river. Here they allowed first a ferry to be set up and later a bridge to be built.

On the opposite side of the river, the site of the City of London, there were two high hills which still exist, although they are difficult to see now under the mass of modern city buildings: Ludgate Hill to the west, today occupied by St. Paul's Cathedral, and Cornhill to the east, the site of the Stock Exchange and the financial and banking center of London. The valley of the Fleet River tributary, running south toward the Thames under the modern Bridge Street and Black-friars Bridge, provided a natural boundary to the west for the new city on the northern bank of the Thames.

There were many other, smaller streams—unpolluted and slow, but free-flowing all year round, they provided a fertile environment for many plants, insects and molluscs. The valleys of these rivers were marshy but the streams themselves ran with clear, fresh water.

And so, though the hills on the north bank provided a suitable environment for settlement, it was the presence of the gravel island on the southern side of the river that dictated where the city would be founded.

Above: No. 10 Downing Street, the official residence of Britain's Prime Minister since 1732, when King George II presented the property to Robert Walpole, Britain's first Prime Minister.
Below: Broadcasting House, spiritual home of the state British Broadcasting Corporation or B.B.C.

CHAPTER 2
THE BEGINNINGS
ROMAN LONDON 43-410

"London: a place not dignified with
the name of a colony, but the chief
residence of merchants, and the great
mart of trade and commerce."

—Gaius Cornelius Tacitus,
The Annals (A.D. 110-120)

London proved the perfect base
for the Roman conquest of
Britain and its unruly inhabitants.
Julius Caesar (right) led the first
invaders from Rome who instantly
started building. Left is a statue,
believed to be of Emperor Trajan,
in front of a section of the Roman
wall that used to extend all the
way around the original "square
mile" of the City of London.

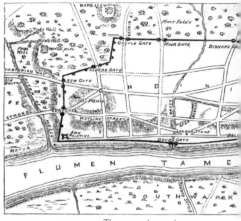

I T WAS JULIUS CAESAR who led the first Roman expedition across the English Channel to Britain in 55 B.C., but the loss of his fleet in a storm forced him to return to France (Gaul) without penetrating any great distance inland. The following year (54 B.C.) he returned and this time advanced as far as the Thames.

The great Roman general recorded that "the river is fordable at one point only and even here with difficulty. At this place I found large enemy forces drawn up on the opposite bank. The bank was also fenced by sharp stakes fixed along the edge, and I was told by prisoners and deserters that similar ones were concealed in the river bed. I sent the cavalry across first and then at once ordered the infantry to follow. But the infantry went with such speed and impetuosity, although they only had their heads above the water, that they attacked at the same moment as the cavalry. The enemy were overpowered and fled from the river bank."

This battle probably took place near modern-day Westminster, the lowest fordable point of the River Thames. From here Caesar advanced to the Iron-Age city (*oppidia*) of Colchester, or Camulodunum, in Essex, and having received the surrender of the local tribes, he returned to France.

Almost 100 years after Caesar's expeditions to Britain, the Romans returned and this time they planned to stay. In A.D. 43 the Emperor Claudius sent four legions with an equal number of auxiliary

The map above shows the walls of Roman London at its greatest extent. This fordable part of the northern bank of the Thames was a logical place to establish a capital for the imperial province. The scheme (left) shows the principal Roman roads of Britain radiating from London. Below is a portion of the dedicatory inscription of a London temple for the state cult of the Roman Emperor.

troops—about 50,000 men—under the command of the general Aulus Plautius to bring Britain completely into the Roman Empire.

Crossroads for the imperial province

London started as a Roman settlement, but its origins were modest and owed everything to the Thames. There is no evidence for a pre-Roman city despite London folklore to the contrary. While there is some evidence for pre-Roman occupation in the London area, such as Iron-Age pottery and a pre-Roman burial from the precincts of the Tower of London, there is no indication that this occupation was ever anything more substantial than small farmsteads.

It was at the first bridging point of the river where the new city would grow. Just seven years after the invasion of Britain, the frontier of this new addition to the Roman Empire had moved northwards, well away from the southeast, and so the conquered territory settled down to enjoy the trappings of Roman civilization.

Colchester had now been raised to the status of a Roman *colonia*, or city, and may have been designated as the provincial capital. A network of roads had been created from the ports in Kent to supply the province. These routes crossed the Thames in the area that

The first Roman army landed at Richborough (Rutupiae) in Kent. After being defeated in a bloody two-day battle on the banks of the River Medway, the Britons withdrew to the Thames, where they waited for the Roman invaders. But the battle of the Thames (in the vicinity of modern Westminster) proved another defeat for the Britons. Outfought and outflanked they were routed. But in the pursuit that followed, many Romans were lost in marshes on the north side of the Thames. Following the battle there was a lull while the Romans awaited the arrival of the Emperor Claudius who, at the head of fresh troops including elephants, led the advance to Colchester. Pictured is a Briton warrior's bronze shield found in the Thames at Battersea.

would become Southwark, probably by ferry, before branching on the northern bank of the river to head east toward Colchester or west and north toward the military frontier. It was around this road network in circa A.D. 50 that the first permanent buildings of London were built, centered on Cornhill, the eastern of the two hills that lie under the modern financial City of London.

Battling the Britons

The first London was a town of single-storey, small-roomed, rectangular buildings of brick-earth bricks and timber, with the occasional Iron-Age "round house" constructed of wattle and daub. There may also have been a few masonry buildings, but these seem to have been rare. London was not, however, a haphazard sprawl created by merchants hoping to cash in on the trade provided by the new regime. Instead, the town was laid out along a grid pattern with distinct property boundaries, which suggests some form of organized town planning.

In A.D. 61 when the Romans tried to absorb the Iceni tribe (based to the east in Norfolk and Suffolk) into the Empire, the Britons rose in opposition. They were led by their queen, Boadicea (more properly Boudicca), and joined by the Trinovantes tribe of the Essex region. Together they attacked the Roman invaders at their stronghold of Colchester and destroyed it, burning the inhabitants alive in the newly-built temple dedicated to the Emperor Claudius.

An attempt by the Roman Ninth Legion to halt the rebels was defeated, and Boadicea's army turned toward the towns of London and St. Albans. The imperial governor, Suetonius Paulinus, who was campaigning in Wales with the bulk of

This modern statue of Queen Boadicea stands opposite the Houses of Parliament. Her army of 100,000 destroyed London in 61 A.D. The Roman historian Tacitus cites Roman and British religiosity that foretold of the coming Roman misfortune: "In the estuary of the Thames had been seen the appearance of an overthrown town; even the ocean had worn the aspect of blood, and, when the tide ebbed, there had been left the likenesses of human forms, marvels interpreted by the Britons, as hopeful, by the Romans, as alarming."

the Roman army, swiftly marched back to the southeast and entered London along the Roman road that lies under modern-day Oxford Street.

The Roman historian Tacitus recorded what happened next: "At first he hesitated whether to stand and fight there. Eventually, his numerical inferiority—and the price only too clearly paid by the rashness of the divisional commander

[who had earlier been defeated by the rebels] decided him to sacrifice the single city of Londinium to save the province as a whole. Unmoved by lamentations and appeals, Suetonius gave the signal for departure. The inhabitants were allowed to accompany him. But those who stayed because they were women or old, or attached to the place, were slaughtered by the enemy. Verulamium [St. Albans] suffered the same fate. The natives enjoyed plundering and thought of nothing else. Bypassing forts and garrisons, they made for where the loot was richest and protection weakest. Roman and provincial deaths at Londinium, Camulodunum and Verulamium are estimated at 70,000. For the British did not take or sell prisoners, or practice other wartime exchanges. They could not wait to cut throats, hang, burn and crucify—as though avenging in advance, the retribution that was on its way." Boadicea was defeated shortly afterwards, but London was completely destroyed.

Pictured right is a reconstruction of the entry to Roman London across the bridge. The large multi-storied building on the right is the basilica with one of the chief temples to the left. No remains of official buildings have been found from the time of the first Roman occupation, but a graveled area near modern-day Fenchurch Street may represent an official marketplace. This was a London populated by artisans and merchants: archaeological finds show that there was substantial trade with the Continent. There is evidence of imported olive oil, wines, Mediterranean grain and fine pottery. But Londoners were also producing their own goods to trade in return. Archaeologists have discovered that there was a mill, a glass-works and even a jeweler's workshop that cut gems. Other evidence suggests that fish were processed on the banks of the Thames, and that gravel was quarried on the edges of the town. To the west, on the further bank of the Walbrook there was a pottery kiln. Tacitus describes London at this time as not being "distinguished by the title *colonia*, but it was an important center for businessmen and merchandise."

From *municipium* to *colonia*

After the rebellion London was rebuilt, and this time it would be far bigger than before. New roads were built and laid out with closely spaced houses and for the first time there was occupation west of the Walbrook valley. A wharf was built out into the river but there is no evidence of a bridge; instead a landing stage was found, suggesting that London at this time was served by ferries.

There is no record of how London was governed in the Roman period but it is possible to make analogies from Roman practices elsewhere. It is difficult to know London's civic status after Boadicea's revolt. However London can probably be classed as a *municipium*, a town that was established by a charter and a constitution based on Rome, but was allowed in addition to retain some native laws.

The inhabitants of a *municipium* were either Roman citizens or had "Latin Rights" allowing them to make contracts and marry Roman citizens. Later London was probably raised to the rank of a *colonia*. This too had a charter and constitution based on Rome, but unlike a *municipium* it retained no native laws.

At the heart of the town, under modern Leadenhall, the Romans built London's first forum and basilica—the focus of Roman civic life. Pictured is a Roman mosaic depicting Bacchus riding on a tiger found in Leadenhall Street. Built to a standard pattern throughout the Empire, the forum was the town's official market place. The forum was an enclosed courtyard: on three sides were building ranges, or wings, containing commercial properties. On the remaining side was the basilica, effectively the town hall. The wings to the east and west of the forum contained a single range of rooms opening onto a rectangular courtyard. To the west of the forum complex was a classical temple, set within its own precinct. Recently discovered further to the south, across Fenchurch Street, is an aisled building of plastered brick walls. It has been suggested that this building was an assembly hall for one of the town guilds.

The trappings of civic life

While the forum and basilica were the focus of civic life, the public baths were often a focus for the town's social life, and were a symbol of the spread of Roman tastes and manners. The baths were places you went to bathe, to exercise, and, just as importantly, to socialize. In fact Roman authorities were constantly trying to ban mixed bathing. In the rebuilding after Boadicea's revolt two bath houses were constructed in London. These were complex buildings, the ancestor of the modern Turkish bath, containing a hot room (*caldarium*), a warm room (*tepidarium*), a cold room (*frigidarium*), and changing rooms (*apoditerium*). In addition, each bath house would have had an exercise area (*palaestra*).

Another symbol of Romanization was the amphitheater. London's was within the city limits in the vicinity of the modern Guildhall. Started between A.D. 70 and 80, the amphitheater consisted of an oval arena surrounded by banks of seats on a timber and earth framework. The entertainment, provided by the town authorities or local dignitaries, would have included gladiatorial combats and shows where animals would be fought or set against each other. When the amphitheater was excavated in modern times, a wooden drain found under the arena contained grisly evidence of the shows held there: it contained five human skull fragments, leg and jaw bones as well as the skull of a bull.

A provincial capital

At some point around the turn of the second century A.D. it was decided to establish the provincial capital at London. Large areas around the forum were cleared of buildings and work began on a new basilica and forum complex. Construction began about A.D. 90 and took 30 years to complete, and by the time it was finished, London's new basilica and

In terms of government, London would have had an *ordo*, or council, made up of 100 *decurions*, or councillors. To become a *decurion* a man would have to be over 30, possess the necessary property or wealth qualifications, reside in or near the town, and enjoy either Roman citizenship or Latin rights. The *decurions* were supposed to be elected by an assembly of the citizens, though in reality the *ordo* often became self-perpetuating. Below is a monument to a man who may have been either a standard-bearer or a retired army officer who held a high civil post.

forum was the biggest north of the Alps.

Running along the northern side of the basilica were two sets of rooms. The first were only accessible from within the basilica. These were offices for the various city officials, and beyond them—accessible only from the street—was a row of shops. While the offices were painted different colors, the shops on the street were almost always red and white.

Elsewhere too there was major rebuilding work. The baths were enlarged and the amphitheater was rebuilt in stone. Work also began on a 12-acre fort to the northwest of the city, at Cripplegate. Constructed between A.D. 90–120, the fort contained four fortified gates in the middle of each of the walls. London was not a garrison town; instead the fort provided accommodation for the Governor's personal troops, a thousand-strong force seconded from all the legions serving in the province.

On the river a new quay was built and, on the new land this created, roads were built as well as buildings that have been interpreted as warehouses and a customs house. Archaeological finds show that London's commercial life was thriving: olive oil, fish sauce, wine, grape syrup (*defrutum*), olives and fine pottery were all imported from France, Spain and the Mediterranean. Related to the new harbor facilities, and perhaps an indication of the rise in London's status, the old ferry crossing was abandoned and a bridge was built linking the banks of the Thames.

London's first bridge was built around A.D. 85–90, and was situated just a few yards downstream of today's London Bridge. It has been calculated that

This inscription in Latin is the oldest physical evidence of London being named as a city. The stone tablet, dating from A.D.150, says in translation: "To the spirits of the emperors and the God Mars Camulos, Tiberinius Celerianus, ranking *moritex* [chief trader negotiator] of the traders of London." As a provincial capital of the Roman Empire, London was the base for the province's Procurator and the Imperial Governor. The Procurator was responsible for collecting taxes throughout the province, while the Governor was the Roman Emperor's direct representative: he had total command of the army, as well as the task of overseeing the economic and physical development of the province.

the bridge was just over 1,000 feet (320 meters) long, and comprised a timber roadway laid on piers across the river. It may have had a central section that could be raised to allow the passage of ships. Finds from the river suggest that there may have been a shrine halfway across.

It was not just on the river where the Romans were changing the physical appearance of the town, they also set about remodelling the marshy tributary streams and their valleys. They canalized the streams with timber walls, and filled the marshy, low-lying valleys with gravel and clay. Over this reclaimed land, two main roads were laid out with new buildings erected along them. Some of these building were domestic, others were workshops, and it seems that this area became an industrial zone. There was a smithy, a boneworker, a glassmaker, and a pottery. There were probably also watermills, but the most common industry of all was leatherworking and tanning.

London's rise in status was also reflected in the town's domestic buildings. New houses were erected on plots that had been vacant since Boadicea's rebellion. Often these houses were of far greater status than before, their rooms decorated with painted plaster walls and tesselated floors. On the south bank of the Thames (today's Southwark), there was a new spate of building and expansion. Wharves were constructed and new domestic and industrial buildings put up.

The evidence suggests that the settlement on the south side of the Thames was no mere

A visit to the baths, such as the Roman complex still preserved in the basement of a building off the Strand, would begin with a plunge in the cold room before moving on to the warm room and finally the hot room, followed by a rub-down. The rooms were heated by furnaces stoked by slaves. The heat and smoke warmed up the rooms through an ingenious under-floor heating system called a "hypocaust." The walls too would be heated by hollow box tiles running up through them.

suburb but an integral part of Londinium. By the end of the second century, the Roman city had expanded far beyond the boundaries of the first-century town. Nevertheless it must still have had a relatively rural feel to it at times. Archaeologists have found evidence of food animals in large quantities such as sheep and cattle bones, and it seems that pigs were not an uncommon sight in the yards of many of the buildings. Wild animals also are represented in the archaeological record: the remains of frogs, snakes, various types of rodent, and deer have been found as well as field and woodland birds, and even a barn owl in the basilica, as well as a host of waterfowl, presumably from the Thames. It seems that beyond the city boundaries was a landscape of farms, woodland and pastures, and several villas are known to have existed in the Greater London area.

Thanks to Latin inscriptions, we know the names of many of the Roman Londoners. This stone sarcophagus, found by Westminster Abbey

bears the name of "Valerius Amandinus." Below is a monument found on Ludgate Hill. A Roman soldier wears a belted tunic and cloak. In his right hand is a dagger while his left holds a scroll. Above him are the words: "To the departed spirits. To Vivius Marcianus, soldier of the Second Augustan Legion, Januaria Martina his most dutiful wife raised this memorial."

Imperial decline and loss of trade

The years between A.D. 90 and 120 can be seen as a time of spectacular growth for London as it turned from a small trading settlement into a provincial capital, but from the mid-second century onwards London as a trading center went into decline.

By the late second century, there is evidence that the area to the west was suffering from depopulation, with many of the workshops being abandoned. This may have been due in part to a devastating fire which swept through the western half of the city some time in the 120s as well as the result of a plague that swept through the Empire between A.D. 165–190.

This period also saw the end of Roman imperial expansion and the loss of many military contracts; instead, trade became more insular, focusing on local production and the countryside rather than international commerce through port towns like London.

But in an apparent contradiction to the signs of

commercial decline there appears to have been a relatively wealthy resident population. There was new building on hitherto green-field plots and some of the old timber and brick-earth buildings were replaced by more substantial masonry structures. There is ample evidence of large urban villas with painted plaster walls, central-heating systems, tessellated pavements and mosaics; one even had evidence of a piped water supply.

At least two new temples were built, an octagonal Romano-Celtic temple near the modern Old Bailey and a temple in the Walbrook valley dedicated to the Persian god Mithras. A new bridge was laid across the River Fleet, and a monumental arch was erected in the southwest of the city possibly along with other new public buildings. But perhaps the biggest single official public work of this period was the construction of the city wall.

The late-second, early-third century was a time of prolific city-wall building throughout Britain. Whether it was the rebellion of Albinus or another factor that caused the building of London's city wall, between A.D. 190 and 220, a two-mile long wall, and 20-feet high was constructed around London. The wall had five main gates, corresponding to the present-day City's Aldgate, Bishopsgate, Newgate, Ludgate and Aldersgate, although this last was probably added later.

Caught up in Rome's turbulence

Sometime in A.D. 197 or shortly after, Britain was divided into two provinces: "Brittania Inferior" in the

Illustrated are Roman remains in Billingsgate discovered by the Thames in the 19th century. There is evidence that there was a significant drop in the level of the river by A.D. 270, perhaps as much as 5ft (1.5m). This effectively meant that, unlike today, the Thames in London ceased to be tidal for a period. This would have had a dramatic effect on London as a port as ships would no longer be able to ride in and out of the city on the ebb and flow of the tide. The period between A.D. 70 and 250 saw frequent building activity on London's riverside with the quay being extended some 162 feet into the river, effectively chasing the Thames as the level dropped.

north, with a capital at York, and "Brittania Superior" in the south with a capital at London. The decades that immediately followed proved turbulent for the Roman Empire, and between A.D. 260 to 274 Britain was part of a breakaway Gallic Empire.

It is difficult to relate the turbulent history of the third century to the archaeology of London. A vast building overlooking the Thames that was begun in A.D. 293-294 may have been intended as a palace for the imperial usurper Allectus, but it was never finished. On the river frontage, the harbor, which seems to have fallen into disrepair by A.D. 270, was cut off from the town during the construction at the end of the century of an extension of the city wall along the river. A watch-tower a few miles downriver at Shadwell was constructed at this time to provide early warning of any Saxon raiders coming up the Thames. On the south bank the industrial workshops were replaced in the mid-second century with substantial residential dwellings, but by the middle of the fourth century these had been abandoned.

Century of change

This was not however a period of total decline: the imperial usurper Carausius established a mint in

In 1954 excavations for the construction of Bucklebury House, an office block in the City of London, uncovered the remains of a large Mithraic temple. The foundations and wall bases of the temple are preserved just as they appeared when uncovered some 18 feet below the surface where the temple would have stood on the original bank of the Walbrook river. The temple was built by the Romans towards the end of the 2nd century A.D. as a place of worship for the deity Mithras, a popular god in the Roman imperial army at this time. The temple would have been an important focus for the cityfolk, just as photographed here today with the Lord Mayor's Parade passing in the background.

London in A.D. 290 and this continued to mint coins till A.D. 326, long after Britain was restored to the Empire. Elsewhere people were constructing high-quality private dwellings. The pattern that emerges is of a town in change rather than decline, of a wealthy citizenry building large town villas within the relative safety of the city walls, and a town authority still capable of undertaking public building works.

The political wars of the Roman Empire during the late third century were eventually brought to an end by the Emperor Diocletian who re-established peace throughout the Empire. Diocletian also revolutionized the way the province was governed. Brittannia Inferior was divided into "Brittannia Secunda" and "Flavia Caesariensis" with provincial capitals at York and Lincoln respectively. Brittannia Superior was divided into "Brittannia Prima" in the west and "Maxima Caesariensis" in the east, with provincial capitals at Cirencester and London respectively. The four provinces together formed the Diocese of Brittannia.

Under these reforms, London was not only the provincial capital of Maxima Caesariensis but also the base of the Vicarius, the home for the imperial treasury and the administrative capital of the whole diocese. Unfortunately the physical evidence for this period of London's history rarely survives. What evidence there is suggests urban decline. The streets had not been resurfaced since the mid-to-late third century, and were becoming rutted with the drainage ditches that flanked them silting up.

At the turn of the fourth century, the basilica and forum were demolished. In fact, there is no evidence at all for any official buildings or public baths from this period. Even the bridge across the Thames may have fallen into disrepair in the first half of the century, perhaps falling down altogether with the river crossing reverting back to a ferry.

After a series of struggles to wrest power back to Rome, in A.D. 296 Britain was invaded by Constantius, one of two Junior Emperors (Caesar) of the Roman Empire. He entered London in triumph after defeating Frankish mercenaries who had been plundering the town. It is possible that London was given the title "Caesarea" in his honor by a grateful citizenry. In 306, he returned, this time with the rank of Senior Emperor (Augustus) and once again London may have been renamed in his honor, this time "Augusta." The two sides of this gold medal commemorate his arrival in London in A.D. 296.

Nevertheless, London was still an important town even becoming a mint for a time in the 380s. There was also some new construction; a group of first-century warehouses in the area of modern-day Pudding Lane were converted into dwellings and a building nearby was rebuilt with a central heating system. In the west of the city the site of the unfinished "Palace of Allectus" was occupied by wooden dwellings, and in the east of the city just to the north of the Tower of London a

Pictured are the crowds of Londoners drawn in 1869 to view a Roman mosaic pavement unearthed during building excavations in Bucklersbury in the City. A luxury private residence was also found at Billingsgate that had its own bath house complex. Because of continuous development over the centuries, the area has been rich in such finds. Nearby, under the present Old Bailey, stood an octagonal temple, demolished in A.D. 270, plus a centrally heated masonry building, perhaps an official inn or staging post (*mansio*).

large aisled building that might have been a cathedral church was found. It is known that a bishop from London attended the Council of Arles in A.D. 314.

Last of the Romans

During the last years of the fourth century the Roman Empire was once again plagued by imperial pretenders and civil wars. In A.D. 350 Magentius, one of these claimants who had considerable support in Britain, made a bid for the throne but by A.D. 353 he had been defeated. In the purge of his supporters that followed, many in Britain whether guilty or not were executed and Marinus, the Vicarius, was forced to commit suicide. At the same time barbarian incursions into the Empire were a growing problem. In A.D. 367 a combined force of Picts, Scots, Saxons and Franks attacked the province. Hadrian's Wall, the fortified northern border of the Roman Empire was overrun.

With the province in chaos, General Theodosius was dispatched with an army to restore order. Theodosius landed in Kent and marched to London; the Roman historian Ammianus Marcellinus described the events: "He quickly routed the Barbarians and wrested from them the plunder that the wretched provincials had lost. He restored everything to its owners except for a small part that he distributed to his exhausted troops, and then entered Londinium in triumph. Hitherto it had been plunged in the deepest distress, but it was now re-established almost before it could have hoped for rescue."

This was a twilight time for the Empire in Britain, and although the Barbarian invasion had been defeated, smaller raids would continue throughout the remainder of the century. The province also suffered during further struggles within the Empire for control. In A.D. 398 the Roman General Stilicho fought a campaign to drive the Barbarians back. The following year he ordered the strengthening of the defenses throughout the diocese. It may be as a result of this order that the last known official Roman construction was carried out in London.

At the beginning of the fifth century, Britain was troubled by more imperial claimants; then in A.D. 407 the usurper Constantine (Constantine III) crossed to France to pursue his claim, taking the army with him. Left without any troops and facing a major Saxon attack, the province of Britain rebelled. In A.D. 410 the Emperor Honorius officially wrote to the citizens of Britain and told them that they had to take responsibility for their own defense—the Romans would not be coming back. After 370 years, Roman Britain had come to an end.

Pictured is a bronze bust of Emperor Hadrian, who built the great coast-to-coast Wall across the north of England to keep the Picts at bay. Found in the bed of the Thames at London Bridge, it is the only portrait bust of a Roman emperor recorded to have been discovered in Britain. Below is an altar to the goddess Diana, found to the northeast of St. Paul's Cathedral.

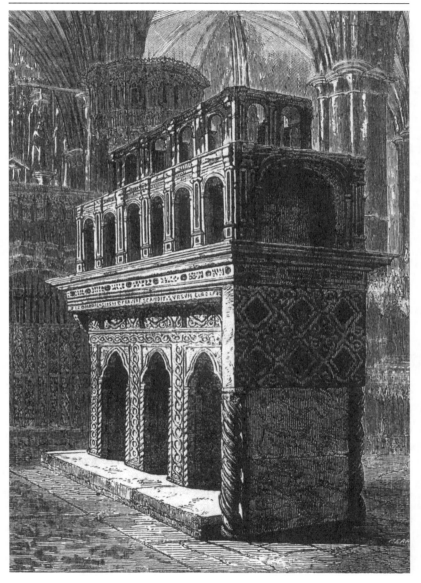

CHAPTER 3

A CITY REBORN
SAXON LONDON 410-1066

"In this year Hengist and Æsc fought against the Britons at a place which is called Crecganford and slew four thousand men; and the Britons then forsook Kent and fled to London in great terror."
—*The Anglo-Saxon Chronicle*, for the Year 457

"The City of London is a mart for many nations who visit it by land and sea."
—The Venerable Bede, *A History of the English Church And People* (731)

Left: The tomb of the Saxon king and saint, Edward the Confessor, in Westminster Abbey.
Right: Head of King Alfred the Great from a silver penny minted during his reign.

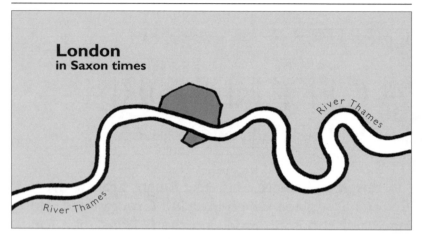

London
in Saxon times

River Thames

River Thames

B
Y 410 BRITAIN WAS EFFECTIVELY
an independent state on the edge of the
ailing Roman Empire. In the two centuries
that followed Roman Britain would be
transformed into Anglo-Saxon England.
As a Roman province, administration had rested on a
network of self-governing regions. Often these were
pre-Roman *civitates peregrinae*, or tribal areas,
governed from a local capital or sometimes these were
created by the grant of land (*territorium*) to a
town or city. It is probable that officials,
soldiers and civil service all departed with the
break from Rome and that the various towns
and territories fragmented into small city-states
and kingdoms. When the Emperor Honorius
officially severed Britain's links with the Empire in
410 he addressed his letter to the people (*civitates*)
and not to an individual successor. Nevertheless, it
does seem that there was some attempt to preserve a
Romanized lifestyle: in 429, when St. Germinus,
Bishop of Auxerre, visited Britain, he was met by
civic leaders and church dignitaries and was taken to
Verulamium to see the shrine of St. Alban.

After the Romans left, it
took two centuries for
the city to recover.
A cross-shaped bronze
brooch found in Tower
Street. From the fifth or
early sixth century, it is
of West Saxon origin.

The history of the post-Roman period is obscure, it is a time shrouded in myth and legend. It was the age of King Arthur and the Knights of the Round Table. One individual known from this period is Vortigern; the name is a Celtic translation of "high king." Vortigern seems to have flourished in the first two or three decades of the fifth century. It was Vortigern, so the historical sources for the period claim, that invited the Saxons to settle in Britain in return for military service. The practice of giving barbarians land in return for their employment as soldiers had been a common practice in the later Roman period and the first Germanic settlement of Britain may actually date from the third or fourth century.

Whatever the circumstance of their settlement, it is quite clear that there was a significant and increasing Anglo-Saxon presence in Kent and the lower Thames valley during the fifth and sixth centuries. This was a time of warfare and co-existence that would ultimately result in the defeat of the Britons and the creation of Anglo-Saxon England.

Collapse of the city

In London there seems to have been a total collapse. No physical evidence has yet been found that London was occupied in the fifth century. Nevertheless, in 457 when the Anglo-Saxons defeated the British in a battle fought at Crecganford (probably Crayford in Kent) the Britons retreated to the protection of the walls of Londinium. By the middle of the fifth century the Anglo-Saxons were well established along the Thames as far west as Reading. Pagan Anglo-Saxon cemeteries have been found in a ring to the south of London from the nearest at Greenwich in the southeast to Ham, Northfleet, Mitcham and Croydon in the southwest; all these cemeteries would have had a nearby settlement.

By the beginning of the sixth century the Anglo-Saxons were well established in the southeast of

On the north side of the Thames pagan cemeteries are not so common. The closest to London is at Hanwell nine miles west of the city. It has been

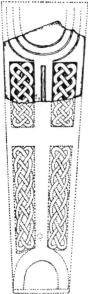

suggested that the absence of settlement-period cemeteries to the north of the Thames combined with the presence of a series of defensive dikes on the Hertfordshire-Middlesex border represents the presence of a *territorium* still administered from London. Pictured above is a portion of a carved 10th-century grave-slab from the churchyard of St. Benet Fink.

England and London was within their sphere of control. Nevertheless the settlers still avoided the Roman city, although they did settle nearby. Traces of late fifth- and sixth-century occupation have been found in Harmondsworth and Hammersmith, and there is evidence for sixth-century occupation near the northern end of the Tottenham Court Road, the closest occupation from this period yet found to the Roman city.

London itself would have had few attractions for the early Anglo-Saxons who were essentially farmers living in small communities and isolated farmsteads. They were certainly fierce fighters and warriors but they had no army, and their style of warfare had little use for the city walls of London. The reasons for London's growth in the Roman period, its status as provincial capital, as well as its river crossing and harbor facilities, had little attraction for the new settlers. The Anglo-Saxons had no need of a capital city, the bridge that had spanned the Thames had almost certainly collapsed and the port had been long since cut off from the city by the defensive riverside wall.

By the end of the sixth century the Anglo-Saxon settlement had stabilized into a series of small kingdoms. In 596 Pope Gregory the Great sent St. Augustine, a Benedictine monk, as a missionary to England to convert the Anglo-Saxons. Augustine was allowed to establish a church in Canterbury by Ethelbert I, king of Kent whose queen was already a Christian.

In 601 the Pope sent more Benedictines with instructions to found bishoprics in York and London. Augustine sent the monk Mellitus to preach to the East Saxons (of Essex) who controlled London. In 604 Saeberht, king of the East Saxons, allowed Mellitus

As in the rest of Europe, the conversion of England was a long

and sometimes violent process as adherents to the older pagan faiths resisted the encroachment of the

new religion. It was a time when saints and martyrs proliferated in almost every area of the Isles. Above is a depiction of the martyrdom of St. Edmund by the Danes. Below are Aldhelm, Hildelith and the Nuns of Barking.

to build a church dedicated to St. Paul in London, of which Mellitus became the first bishop. After King Saeberht died in 616, his sons expelled Mellitus and re-established paganism.

The East Saxons were not reconverted to Christianity until the mission of St. Cedd in 653. In 660 St. Cedd became the Bishop of Essex and it was probably at this time that St. Paul's was refounded. By the time St. Cedd was appointed Bishop of Essex, London had emerged as an Anglo-Saxon *wic* or trading settlement.

Writing in the 730s the Northumbrian monk Bede described London at the turn of the seventh century in his *Ecclesiastical History of the English People*, saying that London "is a trading center of many nations who visit it by land and sea." Known as Lundenwic, the new settlement still avoided the old Roman city, instead it was centered around today's Charing Cross, Trafalgar Square, Covent Garden and the Strand.

The earliest remains from this settlement date to the mid-sixth century and are concentrated in the area around Trafalgar Square. The settlement remained in this area throughout the seventh century, but by the ninth century it had expanded to cover a vast area of about two hundred acres stretching from the Fleet river in the east to Whitehall in the west. The memory of Lundenwic is preserved today in the name Aldwych, literally "Old Wic."

Lundenwic sets up shop

Lundenwic was a trading port; a charter dated to 672-4 refers to "the port of London where ships come to land" and a small quay or harbor from this period was found just to the east of Charing Cross station. Middle-Saxon London was now a frontier town where the kingdoms of Kent, Essex, Wessex and Mercia all met. As a result London was

By the year 550, much of Europe had already been converted to Christianity. But in the British Isles, only Ireland, Western Britain and parts of Scotland, were Christian, and the faith had still to reach outside the former Roman Empire. Over the following two centuries, England and Scotland were converted, by missionaries from Rome, France and Ireland. Germany beyond the Rhine was partially converted too, mostly by English

missionaries. Around 731, the Venerable Bede (pictured) wrote about the English mission in his extraordinary *History of the English Church and People*, and included how St. Augustine began his missionary work in England in 597, going on to become the first Archbishop of Canterbury, still the seat of the Church of England today.

controlled by whichever of these kingdoms was in the ascendant, and each of their kings may have had a Royal Hall or palace in London to control trade.

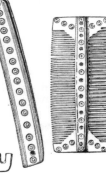

Whether the palace was inside or outside of the city walls it would be incorrect to think of London as a capital. Anglo-Saxon kings were mobile monarchs traveling around their kingdoms. Occasionally they would call a *witan*, or council, to decide laws and policy but these were called to wherever the king was residing at the time. It is known that Anglo-Saxon kings called councils in London, perhaps holding them in the old Roman amphitheater, as was common practice in cities elsewhere in Europe.

Middle-Saxon Lundenwic became a prosperous port enjoying trade with France and Holland, as well as the European interior. In England the trade routes extended along the Thames into Kent, Mercia and Wessex, as well as up the coast to East Anglia. It is known that slaves were exported to Europe from London, finds of loom-weights provide evidence of weaving and the remains of industrial processes show that iron and bronze were being worked. Livestock husbandry may also have been an activity within the settlement.

During the ninth century, Lundenwic was abandoned perhaps because of the increased danger from Viking raids. London was attacked by the Vikings for the first time in 842, the Anglo-Saxon chronicle bluntly recorded "in this year there was

Other evidence for trade in Lundenwic comes from a Law Code of King Hlothere of Kent (673-685) which refers to the king's hall in London where merchants from Kent had to register their

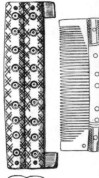

transactions. Anglo-Saxon society could be sophisticated in its tastes, as evidenced by these bone combs and their cases (above) and a girdle tag (below).

great slaughter in London." The Vikings returned in an even greater raid in 851: "the same year came 350 ships to the mouth of the Thames, and stormed Canterbury and London." In 871 the Vikings revisited London and this time they occupied it. By 874 they had taken control of all the Anglo-Saxon kingdoms except Wessex, which they attacked in 875.

Alfred the Great

By 877 Alfred the Great, king of Wessex (the only English king to ever be given the title of "Great") had defeated the Vikings, but in 878, Wessex was again invaded by an army under the command of the Viking leader Guthrun. Again Alfred was victorious and the Vikings were forced to leave his kingdom, but not until Guthrun and thirty of his warriors had been converted to Christianity.

Having driven the Vikings from Wessex, Alfred set about securing his kingdom by creating a system of fortified townships or *burhs* (the origin of the modern word "borough"). In 886 Alfred captured London—the Anglo-Saxon chronicle records: "King Alfred occupied London and all the English people submitted to him, except those who were in captivity to the Danes [Vikings]." King Alfred had become the first king of England, ruling Wessex and unoccupied Mercia; that is, all the land south of a line running from London to the river Mersey. London was now on the frontier between England and that part of England occupied by the Vikings (the Danelaw),

In contrast to the ruined masonary buildings of the old Roman city, most of the buildings in Lundenwic were rectangular wooden constructions often with sunken floors. The walls were of wattle supported by posts set directly into the ground. On the roof would have been thatch or turf. These buildings generally had small yards where rubbish was disposed of by shovelling into pits, old wells or sometimes just dumped

as "middens." Like many other Anglo-Saxon trading settlements of this date, Lundenwic had no walls or defenses. Pictured are golden plates, now in the British Museum, from a rich Saxon household in Sutton Hoo, northern England, similar to those used by rich Saxons in the London area.

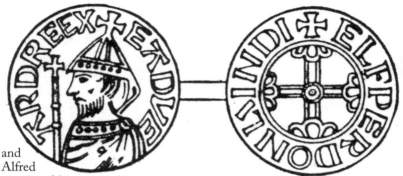

and
Alfred
appointed his son-in-law
Ethelred, a Mercian noble, to administer London and
his Mercian territories.

The City of "Lundenburh"

There may have been some occupation of the old
Roman city in the area round the Anglo-Saxon
cathedral of St. Paul's since the middle of the
seventh century, but now the city was reoccupied
on a much larger scale, the defenses were repaired
and London became the fortified town of
Lundenburh. Southwark on the south bank of the
river may also have been fortified as there is a
reference to the "South Work, the defensive work
of the men of Surrey (*suthringa geweorche*)."

Over the next two centuries, Lundenburh
grew within the Roman city walls. The bridge
was rebuilt over the river, on virtually the same
spot as the Roman bridge, although the Saxon bridge
may date to the late 10th or early 11th century rather
than the 9th. The bridge became an integral part of
the city's defenses and was used to prevent ships from
sailing up the Thames. A new street plan which bore
little resemblance to the regular Roman street grid
was laid out. Only where they were the most obvious
paths to take did the Roman roads survive.

Once again London
became a mint. The first
coins may have been
issued from London by
Eadbald, king of Kent, as

early as the 640s. By
870 there were 15
"moneyers," or coin
minters, working in
London, although it is

not known if coins were
produced inside the old
city walls of Londinium
or in Lundenwic. Pictured
are coins of Edward the
Confessor and William
the Conqueror, found at
the church of St. Mary-
at-Hill.

As well as being a defended settlement Lunden-burh was also a trading community with links to continental Europe. At least one new wharf (*hythe*, the Old English word for "wharf"), that at Queen-hythe, was constructed during the reign of Alfred. There may have been others at New Fresh Wharf just to the east of London Bridge and Billingsgate, both of which can be dated to first years of the 11th century and may well be earlier. Finds of quernstones and pottery show there were trading links to the Rhine-land, and amber, walrus ivory and whet-stones show trade links with the Scandinavian countries.

There were also Anglo-Saxon merchants operating as far away as Italy, exchanging wool, tin and slaves for silk, spices and gold. There were domestic industries and trades too, such as bone, metal, leather and cloth working, as well as trade in foodstuffs, fruit, fish and livestock. Both Lambeth (*lamb hythe*) and Rotherhythe (*rother* is an Old English word for cattle) may have been quays involved with the import and export of livestock. It is recorded in an ordinance dated between 978 and 1035 that farmers had to pay a toll to sell their produce in the market "from hampers with hens, one hen as toll, and from one hamper of eggs, five eggs as toll if they come to market. Women who deal in dairy produce pay one penny two weeks before Christmas and another penny a week before Christmas." The main markets (*ceap* in Old English, pronounced "cheap") in the city were centered on Cheapside and Eastcheap.

London was already becoming an important trade center in the Anglo-Saxon world as shown by the variety of these remains found under the city. Their fine

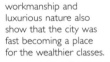

workmanship and luxurious nature also show that the city was fast becoming a place for the wealthier classes.

Beating off the Vikings

By 920 King Edward the Elder, Alfred's grandson, had conquered the Viking lands of the Danelaw to rule the entire kingdom of England. But from the 980s onwards the peace of the kingdom was disturbed by a

renewal of the Viking threat. In 994 a large Viking force under the command of Olaf Tryggvason, the King of Norway, and Swein "Forkbeard," the King of Denmark, attacked London but were beaten off.

In 1009, a Viking force wintering in Kent made forays against the city. *The Anglo-Saxon Chronicle* describes that "they made frequent attacks on the borough of London, but praise be to God, she still stands safe and sound and the Danes always suffered heavy losses there."

In 1013 Swein returned to England, and this time he subdued much of the country and was recognized as king by the Northumbrians and the Danes of Eastern England and East Anglia. In a second campaign he conquered English Mercia and Wessex before moving against London, where the English king Ethelred II the Unready was in residence. Again the city defenses held, and the Vikings were beaten off.

Cnut fights for the Crown

However by the end of the year, with the Vikings in command of much of England, London had little option but to surrender. King Ethelred fled to Normandy and Swein was recognized as king. Swein's success however was short-lived: in February 1014 he died and was succeeded by his son Cnut (Canute).

The Anglo-Saxon Chronicle described the Viking attack on London in 994 as follows: "In this year Anlaf [Olaf] and Swein came to London with 94 ships, and kept up an unceasing attack on the city, and they purposed, moreover, to set it on fire. But there, God be thanked, they came off worse than they ever thought possible." The Scandinavians also left their mark on Britain, as evidenced by the quality of this bronze mount of a reliquary with a runic inscription found in the Thames.

With Swein's death, Ethelred who had formed an alliance with St. Olaf of Norway (king of Norway from 1016-1030) returned from exile at the head of a large army.

Cnut had little option but to withdraw to Denmark. London however was still in Danish hands, and Ethelred and Olaf had to take the city by force. An attack on Southwark was beaten off but later Ethelred's forces were able to attach ropes to the bridge from boats in the river and pull part of it down. Southwark was captured and London surrendered, once again becoming Ethelred's base.

In 1015 Cnut returned with a large army. After a brief campaign south of the Thames he received the surrender of Wessex. In the early months of 1016 he invaded Mercia. Ethelred's son Edmund "Ironside" raised a force to oppose them but the levies refused to go into battle without the king and the forces from London. In 1016 Ethelred died and the council in London proclaimed his son Edmund king, but many of the nobles in Wessex recognized Cnut instead. Edmund now launched a campaign to recapture Wessex—Cnut meanwhile brought his forces up the Thames and laid siege to London. The *Anglo-Saxon Chronicle* records that: "They dug a great channel on the south bank and dragged their ships to the west side of the bridge, and afterwards built earthworks outside the borough so that no one could get in or out and attacked the borough repeatedly but they withstood them valiantly."

King Cnut the Great was an astute politician and Viking warrior who became the ruler of an empire which, at its height, included England, Denmark, Norway and part of Sweden. Below are the two sides of a coin issued earlier by Egbert (829-30). It was the first coin after 800 with the mint name of "LVNDONIA CIVIT(AS)," probably to celebrate West Saxon control of the city.

Edmund marched back to London and lifted the siege, but following a battle at Brentford his losses were so great he had to return to Wessex for reinforcements. Cnut now launched one more major attack on the city, but was beaten off by the defenders and withdrew to East Anglia. In October 1016 Edmund and Cnut fought their last battle at Ashingdon in Essex—Edmund was defeated and made terms. Cnut recognized Edmund as king of Wessex, and Edmund recognized Cnut as king of all the territory north of

the Thames including London. Shortly after the battle Edmund died and Cnut was left as the undisputed king of England.

Forced to pay Danegeld

Cnut's victory came at a high price—he raised a levy (Danegeld) of £83,000 to pay off his forces, £11,000 of which, about five tons of silver pennies, was raised from London. But the struggles of the various belligerents to control London during the wars of 1013 to 1016 illustrate that by the 11th century London had achieved an important status. The city was strategically important, controlling as it did the first crossing point of the Thames as well as the Thames valley itself. Secondly, London offered great wealth to the person who controlled it, evident by the city's ability to pay the Danegeld of 1017/18.

When Cnut died, he was succeeded by his two son: first Harold I "Harefoot" (1035-1040) then Harthacnut ("Half-Cnut," 1040-1042) who died in Lambeth after a particularly heavy drinking bout. On the death of Harthacnut, "the whole nation chose Edward to be king in London."

Edward was the son of Ethelred II and had been invited to England by Harthacnut in 1041 from Normandy where he had spent the last 25 years in exile. Known as "The Confessor" (and later canonized by Pope Alexander III in 1161), the new king brought a Norman influence to court, including in 1044 appointing the Norman Robert of Jumiege as Bishop of London.

Despite his Norman connections, Edward's reign was dominated by Godwin, Earl of Wessex, whose daughter Edith he had married. In 1051 Edward entered into a power struggle with Godwin, who was exiled, only to return in 1053 at the head of a powerful army. Edward was forced to give in to his powerful subject—in the words of the *Chronicle*, "a

There are many accounts of warfare in England during the Dark Ages. Aside from battles between the local kingdoms, bands of armed warriors regularly sailed in from Scan-

dinavia. Many of their swords and hilts have been found in the Thames near Westminster and Temple. The handles show a strong Irish influence in their ornamentation.

great council was summoned outside London, and all the most distinguished men in the land were present. There Godwin set forth his case, and cleared himself before King Edward of all the charges brought against him and his children. Archbishop Robert [Robert of Jumiege, appointed Archbishop of Canterbury in 1051] was declared an outlaw, together with all the Frenchmen, for they were the cause of all the ill feeling which had arisen between him and the king."

Edward the Confessor founds his capital

Following his humiliation in 1053 and perhaps hoping to escape the politics and intrigue of London, Edward moved his palace one and a half miles west of the city to an island created by the Thames and the Tyburn rivers, known as Thorney Island (modern Westminster).

Edward's decision to move his palace outside the city walls established Westminster as a royal and governmental center, leaving the City as the commercial center, a division that continues to the present day. Edward was now 50 years old and began withdrawing from politics, preferring instead to devote himself to religion, expressing his piety by building a vast minster—a church attached to a monastery. When he moved to Westminster it was already home to a monastic community and Harold "Harefoot" had been buried there in 1040.

The church at Westminster may have been originally founded in the eighth century though its early origins are obscure. Nothing now remains of the great minster church that Edward built and dedicated to St. Peter—it was all swept away when Henry III rebuilt Westminster Abbey as a shrine to the Confessor between 1240 and 1272. The only representation of it to survive is an illustration on the Bayeux Tapestry.

What is known was that Edward's minster, which gave its name to the local area Westminster (St. Paul's in London was the "east minster"), was built in the

Ancient burial grounds in London provide many clues to the people who lived there in the Dark Ages. Pictured is a Danish headstone with runic inscriptions found in St. Paul's churchyard. The central animal motif— particularly the interlaced extension of the limbs —is common in the art of Northern Europe during the eighth century. Other chracteristic features of the period are the spiral attachment of the limbs to the trunk of the animal, the termination of one foot in a redundant head, and the so-called union-knot at the upper angles of the panel. This last motif was originally a device for uniting the ends of the scroll with carried the inscription on Scandinavian tombstones, but here is merely an ornament and seems to have been derived from Ireland.

Norman style by Norman craftsmen, and was the only major Anglo-Saxon church not to be rebuilt after the Norman conquest. William of Malmsbury, writing in the 12th century, said of it: "it was the first in England to be erected in the fashion which all now follow at great expense." The minster was consecrated on December 28, 1065, but the old King was too ill to attend and died on January 6, 1066. He was buried in his great church.

William conquers England

On Edward's death the throne passed to his brother-in-law and Godwin's son, Harold, who was crowned King Harold II on the same day the old king died. The coronation took place in Edward's minster church, so beginning a tradition that continues to the present day. Every English monarch has been crowned in Westminster Abbey with the exception of Edward V and Edward VIII, neither of whom had a coronation. However there were other claimants to the throne, including King Harald III "Hardrada" of Norway and Duke William "the Bastard" of Normandy. Hardrada was the first to stake his claim, landing in Yorkshire in September 1066, only to be defeated and killed by Harold's army at the battle of Stamford Bridge. But Harold had virtually no time to celebrate his victory before news came to him that

The funeral procession of Edward the Confessor bearing his body in 1066 to Westminster Abbey— the church he had built. His tomb still exists in the Abbey, behind the high altar. Ten months after his death and the death of his successor Harold, William was crowned king of England in the Abbey, thus starting the tradition of its use ever since as the coronation church of the monarchy. Some time after Edward's death, monks in Westminster made claims that the king had performed miracles, touching people to heal them. King Henry II later saw political advantages in strengthening the memory of Edward. He petitioned for Edward's canonization. The Pope obliged in 1161. And so, 95 years after his death, Edward became a saint.

William of Normandy had landed on the south coast.

The armies of Harold II and William met in battle at Hastings on October 14, 1066. Harold was defeated and killed; he had been on the throne for only nine months. William, now dubbed "the Conqueror," took time to secure Kent before he marched on London. London however held out against him and William contented himself to burning Southwark before moving on to Winchester to seize the English treasury.

Meanwhile in a hastily convened witan in London, Edgar "Aetheling," the great nephew of king Edward, was proclaimed king. *The Anglo-Saxon Chronicle* records that "Archbishop Ealdred [of York] and the citizens of London wished to have Prince Edgar for king, as was indeed his right by birth, and Edwin and Morcar [earls of Mercia and Northumbria respectively] promised that they would fight for him, but always when some initiative should have been shown there was delay from day to day until matters went from bad to worse."

There was no attempt to organize a coronation for Edgar and when William crossed the Thames at Wallingford and began to ravage the territory north of London the city surrendered to him. The surrender took place at Berkhampstead, and the *Chronicle* records the event: "There he [William] was met by bishop Ealdred, Prince Edgar, Earl Edwin, Earl Morcar, and all the best men from London who submitted from force of circumstance… they gave him hostages and swore oaths of fealty, and he promised to be a gracious lord to them."

Anglo-Saxon England had come to an end.

William of Normandy's claim to the English throne was the result of strong links with the English nobility. When Edward the Confessor was in his teens, the Danes had invaded England and removed his father from the throne. Edward fled to Normandy, which was ruled by his uncle. The Saxon Edward therefore spent a large part of his life in Normandy and came under the influence of the Normans. He kept his nation at peace but favored Normans over Saxons. His successor, Harold II—the last Saxon king of England—immediately had to deal with a number of challengers to the throne during his brief, nine-month reign. Claiming that Harold had recognized him as heir to the English throne while shipwrecked in Normandy two years earlier, William invaded England in the south just as Harold was defeating the Vikings near York, in the north.

CHAPTER 4
THE NOBLE CITY
MEDIEVAL LONDON 1066-1536

"Among the noble cities of the world that Fame cel-
ebrates, the City of London of the Kingdom of the
English, is the one seat that pours out its fame more
widely, sends to further lands its wealth and trade,
lifts its head higher than the rest."

—William FitzStephen,
The Life of Thomas à Becket (c. 1180)

Pictured left is a panorama of Medieval
London showing the Thames winding
around the Tower of London. In the
background can be seen old London
Bridge, the spire of St. Paul's Cathedral
and the tower of Westminster Abbey.
Right is a depiction of the Parliament
of Edward I (r. 1272-1307) with King
Alexander of Scotland on his left and
Prince Llywelyn of Wales on the right.
The forceful ruler was named after the
Saxon Edward the Confessor and
became known as the "Hammer of the
Scots" after a series of long campaigns
in Scotland.

WILLIAM THE CONQUEROR was crowned king at Westminster Abbey on Christmas Day, 1066. But the ceremony was marred when the king's Norman-French bodyguard confused the congregation's cries of support with the noise of a riot. Alarmed they set fire to the gates of the abbey and some of the nearby buildings. In the chaos that followed it was said that the new king was visibly shaken: for the first time in his life, he trembled from head to foot. William was perhaps understandably nervous, for he must have known that the citizens of London had only surrendered to the Norman invaders when they had no option to do otherwise, and gladly would have rid themselves of him.

London, however, was the key to the possession of the kingdom. The new king had to both subdue London and gain its support. In a gesture of friendship at the time of his coronation, William issued a charter to London.

He told them: "William, King, greets William, Bishop and Godfrey, Portreeve, and all the burghers within London, French and English friendlike. And I give you to know that I will that you be worthy of all the laws you were worthy of in the time of King Edward. And I will that every child shall be his father's hereafter his father's day. And I will not suffer any man to do you wrong. God preserve you."

Yet the new regime also needed to control London, so following his coronation William withdrew to Barking Abbey "while certain

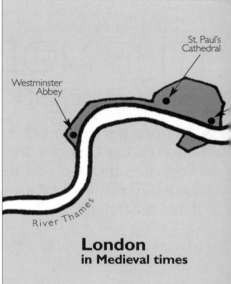

St. Paul's Cathedral

Westminster Abbey

River Thames

London
in Medieval times

In some ways the medieval history of London can be said to have begun on Christmas Day, 1066, when William the Conqueror was crowned king of England. By the early 12th century the population of London was about 18,000, compared to the 45,000 estimated at the height of Roman Britain.

AD

fortifications were made against the fickleness of the vast and fierce population."

A trio of Norman castles

The Conqueror built three castles in London. One was on the eastern bank of the River Fleet and fronting the Thames: this was called Castle Baynard. Another just to the north, was Mont-fitchet Tower, although little is known about this fortification. In 1275, both Castle Baynard and Montfitchet Tower were demolished after they were given to the Archbishop of Canterbury for the foundation of a church and house for the Dominican Blackfriars (after whom that area of London is now named).

The Conqueror built his third castle in the southeast angle of the Roman wall, enclosing the other two sides with a bank and ditch to make a fortified enclosure of about one and a quarter acres. Within this enclosure, work started on a stone tower, which is known today as the White Tower and which lies at the heart of the Tower of London.

King William's rule was based on conquest even after the Battle of Hastings. In order to stay in power, he relied on the loyalty of the knights and soldiers he had brought with him from Normandy. These were well equipped and highly trained for this purpose, but William had to tread carefully and reward them with prizes of English lands to ensure that they stayed loyal. They soon became powerful barons who relished their independence and exercised control over most of the kingdom—and it took a strong king to stand up to them. The Norman conquerors have always been roundly hated by the English. Characters such as Robin Hood, Ivanhoe, and Hereward the Wake, all set in the reign of the Norman Kings, were to suffer to one degree or another because of the "evil" Normans.

Tower of London

River Thames

ELIVM: CON TRA: ҺAROL DVM·REGE: HIC

The construction of the White Tower was overseen by Bishop Gandulf of Rochester, and work probably began soon after 1077. The Tower is still an imposing building: not quite square, it measures 118ft by 97ft and stands 90ft high to its battlements. Constructed mainly of Kentish ragstone, the decorative features of the building were originally of imported Norman Caen stone—most of this was replaced by Portland stone in the 18th century. Originally the building had only two floors over a basement with a pitched M-shaped roof, but during the reign of Henry I (1100-1153), the gables of the roof were hidden by an encircling wall and passage. This wall gave the impression of an additional floor, and the use of decorative windows at top-floor level added to the illusion. A third floor would not be inserted until 1490. The entrance was on the southern side of the building at the top of a flight of wooden stairs. Inside large fireplaces heated the rooms and there was a magnificent chapel for the use of the monarch.

It has been suggested that the White Tower was designed more as a ceremonial residence than as a military building. The large entrance doorway, for example, is undefended, the building contains only residential rooms, and without kitchens food always must have been brought in from outside. Nevertheless the Tower was a statement of William's power and its relevance as an imposition of the new order would not have been lost on Londoners.

Storms and fire

With the exception of his three castles, London probably changed very little in the initial aftermath of the Norman Conquest. However, while William I and his successors may not have intended to rebuild the Saxon city, events often forced them to. In 1090, for example, London was hit by a terrible storm that destroyed over 600 houses, tore the roofs off churches and damaged London Bridge.

Of even greater danger to the city was fire. Writing in the 1170s, William Fitzsteven believed that "the only pests of London are the immoderate drinking of fools and the frequency of fires." London suffered serious fires in 1077, 1086, 1092, 1100, 1133 and one in 1135 that totally destroyed London Bridge. Attempts to prevent fire included a City Ordinance of 1189 that encouraged the building of stone "party walls" between buildings, and in the 1270s, Alderman Arnold fitz Thedmar wrote: "It should be remembered that in ancient times the greater part of the city was built of wood, and the houses covered with straw and stubble, and the like. Hence it happened that when a single house caught fire, the greater part of the city was destroyed through such conflagration; a thing that took place in the first year of the reign of King Stephen [1135]. After this, many of the citizens, to the best of their ability to avoid such a peril, built stone houses upon their foundations covered with thick tiles, and protected against the fury of the flames."

In the fire of 1086, St Paul's Cathedral, only just rebuilt after a fire of 961, was destroyed, along with "many other churches and the largest and fairest part of the whole city." Construction of a new St. Paul's was begun almost immediately. Built of Caen stone, the new church was massive. Stow, recording the building of the cathedral described it as a "work that men of that time judged would never

The Normans built the new cathedral of Old St. Paul's and by 1313 additions made it the third longest church in Europe at 596 feet. The following year the spire was completed—at 489 feet it was the tallest in all Europe. The cathedral became a centrer of trade, with merchants selling their wares and lawyers negotiating in the nave of the church itself, which also became a useful short-cut from the streets outside. In 1660, Charles II appointed Christopher Wren to undertake major repairs to the building but no sooner had Wren begun his work than the Great Fire of London of 1666 reduced Old St. Paul's to nothing but charred timbers and rubble.

have been finished, it was to them so wonderful for length and breadth."

The king's authority

London was also served by a network of local parish churches. By the 12th century the pattern of parishes within the city walls was in existence and the majority had developed before 1066.

Between the Norman Conquest and the end of the 12th century there was also a rapid increase in the number of monastic houses in London.

Following the surrender of London, William the Conqueror chose Westminster Abbey for his coronation, setting a precedent followed by every English monarch since. The king also took over Edward the Confessor's palace. This became a favorite of his heir William II "Rufus," who in 1097 built a great hall on the site. Rufus's Hall was the largest in Europe. Little now remains of his building—the hall had to be restored after a fire in 1291 and was substantially rebuilt by Richard II in the 1390s.

When they were in England, the Norman kings would hold court at Westminster every Whitsun, and William I called two Great Councils (*Curia Regis*) there in 1076 and 1084, but Westminster was in fact only one center

St. Katherine's-by-the-Tower, Holy Trinity Priory at Aldgate, St. Bartholomew's Priory and its hospital at Smithfield, on the south of the Thames, St. Mary Overie (now the Cathedral of St. Saviour, Southwark) and the hospital of St. Thomas, as well as the great Abbey at Bermondsey, were all founded in the late 11th or 12th centuries.

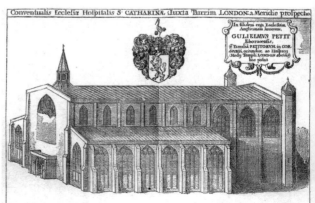

of royal power. There were other equally important palaces in Gloucester and Winchester where kings would spend Christmas and Easter respectively.

The Norman kings and Angevins who followed them had no need for capital cities. They governed their kingdom personally and where they went the government went with them. Only the king's treasury remained in one place, and that was Winchester, not Westminster. But as England evolved from a feudal kingdom to a nation-state the process of government became more bureaucratic and the king increasingly devolved duties to officials in his household. These officials and their staff were the origins of the modern Departments of State.

As the work of these departments grew it was more convenient for them to operate from a permanent base rather than following the king. The first of these departments to settle in one place was the Court of Exchequer. The Treasury itself was moved from Winchester to the headquarters of the Knights Templar on the

Two of the new monastic sites in London belonged to orders of warrior monks. These were the Order of St. John in Jerusalem, founded in Clarkenwell in about 1100, and the Knights Templar (left) who were brought to Britain by Henry I. The Templar's first church was in Holborn but in 1162 they built a monastery and church on the bank of the Thames between London and Westminster, giving the area the name "Temple." Their church with its characteristic circular nave (based on the Holy Sepulchre Church of Jerusalem) still survives.

Strand, eventually moving in 1356 to the purpose-built Jewel Tower in the grounds of the Palace of Westminster.

The Exchequer conducted its business in the great hall of William II, and the clerks were housed nearby. At the head of the Exchequer was the Chief Justicier, who also had responsibility for the law. By the late 1160s a corps of professional judges, lawyers and clerks had become established at the Exchequer, known as the Court of Common Pleas or Court of Common Bench. Here the justices would sit to hear complaints and pass judgement, it was from their decisions that English Common Law developed.

The next office to get a permanent base was the Chancery. By the 13th century, the Chancellor was perhaps the most important official of the king: originally responsible for writing writs or charters, he would accompany the king as he traveled.

However, as the workload of the Chancery increased, the many clerks and scribes and their growing collection of records became less portable. In 1290 Edward I

The Court of Exchequer was an accounting office responsible for the expenditure and receipts of the Treasury. Royal officials were required to attend the Court of Exchequer twice a year to render payments and account for any monies spent. It was far more convenient if this office and its records were based in one place. Westminster, close to London but not controlled by it, with its good communications to the rest of the country, its large royal palace and the great abbey, was an obvious choice for the permanent home of the Exchequer, which was certainly there by 1199.

(1272-1307) gave the Chancery a building in Chancery Lane for the storage of their records.

Parliament finds a home

With the Law Courts, the Exchequer and Chancery all finding homes at Westminster, it was only natural that Parliament should find a home there too. Before the 13th century English kings governed without a Parliament—instead, when there were important matters to discuss, the king would summon a Great Council (*Curia Regis*) to be attended by all the nobility. Unlike Parliament, the Curia Regis was not a forum for discussion, it was a means of enforcing the king's will. However, from the end of the 12th century to the middle of the 13th, the nature of the great council changed, and the nobles (the Lords) began to see themselves as representatives of the whole kingdom.

By 1269 the institution of Parliament had become established and was recognized by Edward I. In the early 14th century the young Parliament split into two chambers as the Squires from the country and the Burgesses from the towns came together to represent their shared interests in a lower house (the Commons) as opposed to the aristocratic members of the upper house (the Lords). Although Parliament preferred Westminster for its meetings, it only was called in time of need and would meet wherever the king was in residence.

The Court of Common Pleas sent justices throughout the country to hear cases locally, though a case could be transferred to Westminster. Although the court was supposed to sit with the king wherever he was in England, in reality after 1188 it rarely left Westminster, and in 1215 it was agreed in Magna Carta that it would be based there permanently. Despite the Chancery, the Exchequer and its courts remaining at Westminster, they were still part of the king's personal government, so when Edward I embarked on his campaigns in Scotland he moved them all to York where they remained until 1338. Pictured is the Court of the King's Bench in the time of Henry VI.

Westminster's royal links

It was Edward III (1327-1377) who established Westminster as the national capital. In 1338, the king launched the Hundred Years War against France, and moved the Exchequer, Court of Common Pleas and the Chancery back to Westminster "where it might be nearer to him in the parts beyond the sea." Of the 51 Parliaments and Councils called by Edward after 1337, only three were held outside Westminster or London.

The growing importance of Westminster attracted the rich and powerful. William Fitzstephen wrote, "nearly all the bishops, abbots, and magnates of England are,

as it were, citizens and freemen of London; having their own splendid houses, to which they resort, where they spend largely when summoned to great councils by the king or by their metropolitan, or drawn thither by their own private affairs."

While Westminster's links with the monarchy had been strengthened and its place as the center of government had been confirmed in the period between 1066 and 1338, the leading citizens of London had ambition to achieve a certain amount of independence from the king. From the early 12th century Londoners were constantly seeking recognition of their "Commune." What the citizens of London wanted was the right to choose their own

At first Parliament had to meet wherever there was space in Westminster Abbey or the palace nearby, but it eventually became customary for them to meet in the "Painted Chamber" of the palace and later in Westminster Hall. The Commons met in the abbey chapter house and after 1380 in the monks' refectory. In the 1340s the King's Council established a Court at Westminster in the Star Chamber (Court of the Star Chamber). By 1345 the Court of Chancery was sitting in Westminster, as was the Court of King's Bench from the mid 1360s. In 1361 the Great Wardrobe, the office responsible for the provisioning of the kings household was established in a building near Baynard's Castle (below) where the Fleet flows into the Thames.

sheriff and justice and to administer their own financial and judicial matters without royal interference. In addition they asked that their tax to be set at £300 (instead of £500), and to be excused certain taxes altogether especially those levied on their trade goods, as well as dispensation from murder

fines (a fine payable by the community for an unsolved murder) and any other fines that might exceed £5.

They wanted an end to the "billeting" of the royal household in the city, to trial by combat, and to penalties imposed for technical errors committed during meetings of the hustings or folkmoot. Lastly, they wanted to ensure that that the citizens and churches of London would be able to enjoy the revenues of their lands, and that their ancient hunting rights in the forests of Middlesex, Surrey and the Chilterns be respected. Only the king could give London this status, and it was claimed by Londoners that Henry I had done just that in the 1130s.

The Commune establishes itself

The first real chance to achieve the Commune of London came in 1135 when Henry I died without a male heir and a bitter struggle for succession to the throne followed. As the barons in Normandy argued over who should take the vacant throne, the citizens of London who

The Mauduit family, the king's hereditary chamberlains, had purchased land to the west of Westminster Abbey by 1200, but many of the new buildings erected clustered instead to the east along the Strand, the riverside road joining Westminster to London, such as York House the palace of the Bishop of Norwich built in 1237, Durham House built in the early 13th century by the Bishop of Durham, Essex House (built 1313) home of the Bishop of Exeter, and the Savoy Palace built in the mid-13th century by the Count of Savoy, uncle of Henry III, and rebuilt in 1345-70 by Henry Duke of Lancaster on the profits he made from the Hundred Years War. Another palace nearby was York Place in Whitehall, which was later taken over as Whitehall Palace by Henry VIII. The Archbishop of Canterbury built his official residence, Lambeth Palace (pictured), across the river from Westminster in 1200, and the Bishop of Winchester had his residence, Winchester Palace, in Southwark, part of his diocese opposite the city in 1109.

had been instrumental in recognizing the legitimacy of monarchs in 1016, 1042 and 1066 now claimed that they had the right and privilege to elect the king whenever the succession was in doubt. They now chose to exercise this right on behalf of Stephen Duke of Mortain and Boulogne, the greatest landowner in England, and recognize him as king in return for his promise to bring peace to the kingdom.

Stephen seems to have accepted

the Commune in London and in return he was never deserted by the city. In 1139, the country was plunged into civil war when Henry's daughter, the Empress Matilda, landed in England to pursue her claim to the throne. Matilda's forces captured Stephen in 1141 and, having obtained the support of the Constable of the Tower, Geoffrey de Mandeville, she was confident enough to enter London for her coronation. But her attempts to raise a tax from the City increased resentment against her, and as an army led by Stephen's queen approached Southwark, the population of London rose up, ejected Matilda from the city and restored Stephen.

When Stephen died in 1154, he was succeeded by

In King John's reign, a group of northern barons marched on London and seized the capital in May 1215. They were therefore able to dictate terms to John and in June he agreed to Magna Carta's 63 clauses outlining the rights and responsibilities of the crown and its principal subjects. John signed the historic charter at Runnymede, on the banks of the Thames upstream of London.

Matilda's son who became Henry II (1154-1189). Henry recognized many of the privileges claimed by London—however, he did not accept the right of the City to elect its own sheriff and justice, and he also raised taxes there.

The first Lord Mayor

Henry II's successor Richard I (1189-1199) showed no signs of granting London any more rights than his father. But in 1190, when Richard, known as "the Lionheart," joined the Third Crusade in Palestine, there was a power struggle in England between the Chancellor Longchamp and the king's brother John. Longchamp was also Constable of the Tower but failed to rally London in his support. Instead this was given to John when he agreed to support the Commune, and he was duly recognized by the citizens of London as the heir presumptive.

With the grant of the Commune in 1191, the office of Lord Mayor was created. Henry FitzAilwin became the first to hold the post that he occupied until his death in 1212. When King Richard finally returned from the Crusades after years of absence, he was unable to suppress the new government in London that had grown used to the absence of a king. When his younger brother John (1199-1216) came to the throne he was prepared to allow London to retain its mayor for a payment of £2,000.

But it was not until the Barons' Revolt in 1215 that John, in a desperate attempt to gain the support of London, issued on May 9, 1215, a charter granting London the right to annually elect its mayor. Despite this the city fell to the barons eight days later without a struggle.

With the barons in possession of

The City's most famous mayor was Richard Whittington, four times between 1391-1419, and whose cat is remembered above. However, his predecessor Henry FitzAilwin (in office 1193-1212; below) was just as illustrious.

London, John was forced to submit and agree to the demands that they set out in the Magna Carta. Among these historic demands was the recognition of the rights and liberties of London. But London

remained in the hands of the barons and when John failed to implement many of their demands, they invited the Dauphin Louis, the son of King Philip II of France, to invade and take the English crown. It was only John's death in 1216 that prevented the French invasion.

Rebels at the gates

London and Westminster had emerged during the Middle Ages as two great centers of power and authority, and there was competition between them that frequently could turn to violence.

Both the City and Royal authorities took measures to curb such violence and public disorder. Each ward was responsible for its own policing but the whole city could be held liable for failures in law enforcement. King William I introduced an 8 o'clock curfew but this fell into disuse after the death of his successor William II.

Sometimes London became involved in more serious violence. In 1381 resentment against a poll tax imposed to pay for the war in France boiled over into rebellion in the counties of Kent and Essex. Known as the Peasants' Revolt, this uprising involved a large force of rebels, estimated by some at 60,000 strong,

In the summer of 1222, a team from the City beat a team from Westminster in a wrestling match. The return match was played in Westminster, but the Steward of the Abbey armed his team and they attacked the Londoners, injuring many of them. As a result, a mob from London attacked Westminster. The Steward's house was pulled down, and when the Abbot of Westminster came to the city to complain, his horse was seized, his servants were attacked, and he was stoned. The Mayor of London was promptly summoned to the Tower by the Chief Justicier and held to account for the disturbance. The City was fined for "disturbing the King's Peace" and three of the ringleaders were hanged. Others were punished with the loss of hands or feet. Competition between the guilds and trades of London (some of their shields are shown, left) could also end in severe violence and even loss of life. As one of many examples, in 1327, there was a serious riot caused by rivalry between the saddlers and the joiners, painters and lorimers. By the time order was restored several people had been killed and many others injured.

who moved on London, where they hoped to gain redress of their grievances. When the rebels arrived, the gates of London were shut but they had supporters in the city. The chroniclers tell us that the Londoners asked themselves: "Why are these good people not allowed to enter the city? They are our people, and all that they do is for us!" And with that, the gates of London were opened for them. Once in the city, the rebels ransacked and burned the palaces. They broke open the prisons of Fleet, Marshalsea and Newgate, freeing the inmates. Tax collectors and lawyers were murdered by the mob, so too were foreign, mainly Flemish, merchants.

King Richard II (1377-1399), though only 14 years old, arranged to meet the rebels at Mile End to the east where he agreed to their demands. Despite the king's concessions the rebels still did not disperse and Richard was forced to meet them the following day at Smithfield by the city walls. This time, Wat Tyler, the rebel leader, behaved insolently toward the young king, toying with his dagger and using insulting words to the monarch's entourage. Outraged by the rebel's behavior, William Walworth, the Lord Mayor of London, stabbed Tyler and mortally wounded him. With that the king took command of the situation by riding toward the rebels shouting: "Sirs, will you shoot your king? I am your captain, follow me!"

During the reign of Edward I, the curfew was reintroduced. At the hour of curfew all the city gates were closed and the drawbridge on London Bridge was raised, the taverns had to close and crossing the river by boat was forbidden. The curfew was enforced by patrols organized by each ward—only respectable citizens or their servants were allowed to go out after the curfew and then only with reasonable cause. The curfew bell is still rung every night at 8 o'clock in the Bell Tower at the Tower (arrowed on the plan, left), probably the last such bell in the city. Anybody caught breaking the curfew risked time in the Cornhill Tun, a prison built expressly for the purpose. For other offenses there were various punishments depending on the crime ranging from prison or execution to a fine or public humiliation in the pillory. Felons could always seek sanctuary in one of the city churches or monastic houses, here they would be safe from arrest, but had to make the choice between facing trial or having their possessions and property confiscated.

The rebels dispersed without further incident. William Walworth was knighted for his part in the affair and the flag of London, the flag of St. George, was given a dagger in the top left corner to commemorate the event.

City under siege

The Peasants' Revolt of 1381 was not the only time that rebels were allowed to enter the city. In 1450, supporters of a demonstration against corruption in government led by John Cade opened the gates of the city to rebels. In a repetition of the events of 1381, the rebels gained entry into the Tower and killed Lord Say, the Lord Treasurer, and William Crowmer, the Sheriff of Kent. For three days the rebels rampaged unchecked through the city until Lord Scales, the Constable of the Tower, led the City militia against them. After a battle on London Bridge the rebels were forced to agree to a truce and dispersed.

The defenses of London were formidable obstacles to any force that did not enjoy the support of the citizenry. But these defenses were never really tested against a professional army. The closest London ever came to a siege was in 1471, during the Wars of the Roses, a civil war between the two rival dynasties of York and Lancaster that claimed the throne for Edward IV and Henry VI respectively. On May 4 the Lancastrian army was defeated at

Pictured below are King Richard II and his council landing from their barge on the Thames to parlay with the rebels of the Peasants' Revolt. The teenaged Richard rode out from the Tower of London with the support of his noblemen, to nearby Mile End. It was here, that he met with the rebel leader, Wat Tyler. After the Lord Mayor killed Tyler, the rebels started an attack, but the young king bravely rode out to them. The rebels followed him and so ended the revolt. This ability of Richard's to make good judgments was not fated to last, however, and his reign ended in turmoil.

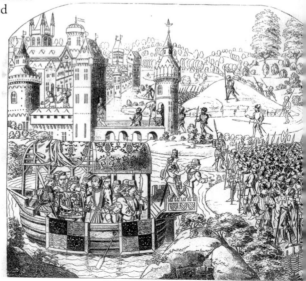

Tewkesbury. At the same time as these events, a squadron of Lancastrian ships sailed up the Thames and demanded safe passage through London so that they could go to the aid of Henry. The Lord Mayor refused. In response, the fleet laid siege to the city and seized Southwark, ranging warships along the Thames. However, their land troops were unable to cross London Bridge as the drawbridge was raised. Instead they broke into the city on the north side of river through Aldgate, but when the portcullis of the gate was closed behind them they were trapped and defeated. After an unsuccessful attempt to destroy the bridge with gunfire, Henry's ships withdrew. On May 27, the new king Edward IV was able to make a triumphal entry into London, and the unfortunate Henry VI was murdered in the Tower.

London is a port and the river has always been filled with craft carrying goods and passengers up and down the River Thames. Some were warships, such as the magnificent Ark Royal built later during Elizabeth I's reign at Deptford and which fought against the Spanish Armada. Upstream, locks keep the water deep, slow moving and navigable. Permanent locks started to be introduced in the 15th century. This process of "modernization" was only finally completed in 1938!

"Queen of the whole country"

To those approaching medieval London from the country the city must have been a fantastic sight. The anonymous author of the *Life of King Stephen* (*Gesta Stephani*) even went as far as describing the city as "the metropolis and queen of the whole country." The city had been growing in wealth and status throughout the Middle Ages and her population had expanded from an estimated 14,000 to 18,000 at the time of the Norman Conquest to between 40,000 and 50,000 by 1340. London was the greatest city in the kingdom, far larger and wealthier than the other great cities of York, Norwich and Bristol.

Viewed from the hills to the north London must have been an impressive sight: the great walls rising over 30 feet on their Roman foundations ran for two miles from the Tower of London in the east to the river Fleet in the west. The wall had six gates that gave access to the city, but also could have other roles. The gates at Newgate and Ludgate were used as prisons. The walls enclosed a square mile of densely populated and crowded city where land was at a premium despite the fact that between 1100 and 1500 the river frontage was pushed southward and a strip of land up to 350 feet (102 meters) wide was reclaimed from the river.

Within the walls London had more than one hundred churches, nine monasteries, several schools, countless small shops and by the 1380s about two hundred inns. Two buildings dominated medieval London: St. Paul's Cathedral and the Tower. By the end of the 13th century, St. Paul's was one of the biggest cathedrals in England—far bigger than the cathedral that replaced it after the Great Fire. Its wooden spire was covered with lead and at 520 feet (153 meters) it was the tallest spire ever built. As well as that of spiritual center, St. Paul's also played a key secular role in London life. The nave was a short cut between Ludgate and the City, and it became a common public meeting place, especially for

The poet Geoffrey Chaucer lived above Aldgate in the City walls between 1374 and 1386 while he was employed as a Comptroller of Petty Customs. His *Canterbury Tales* related the stories told by pilgrims (below) setting off from Southwark to Canterbury Cathedral.

lawyers, who would meet their clients there. It was also used as a market where tradesmen could sell their goods and scriveners could be found to write out documents for a fee. In 1385, the Bishop even complained that Londoners played ball in the nave and shot birds in the churchyard.

Expansion of the Tower

If St. Paul's reminded Londoners of God's authority, the Tower reminded them of the king's. By the middle of the 13th century the Tower was the only survivor of the three castles built by William the Conqueror. It was situated in its own territory or "Liberty," an area of land under the direct jurisdiction of the castle. The Constable of the Tower, who controlled the castle, was a powerful royal official. It was only after securing the support of the Constable, Geoffrey Mandeville, that the Empress Matilda had dared to enter the city in 1141.

From the reign of Henry I onward, successive monarchs, recognizing the importance of a royal citadel in London, have left their mark on the castle. Expansion of its walls with twelve towers effectively doubled the size of the original castle and made it one of the most powerful castles in the country.

While the Tower was primarily a royal citadel and palace, it was also home to the royal mint, the Crown Jewels and, from the

Most Londoners lived in timber-framed houses on stone foundations, bricks did not become common until the 15th century when they were used for fireplaces and chimneys. The houses were built gable-end onto the street and were often two or three stories high, their floors projecting out over the street, sometimes by as much as 5 feet. In the center of the city where land prices were high, houses could be even taller, having up to five stories. The wealthy lived in great mansions usually arranged around a central courtyard, service buildings faced onto the street with the living accommodation to the rear.

13th century to the 19th, the home of the Royal Menagerie, or Zoo. Most famously, perhaps, the Tower was a state prison—and on occasion, a place of execution.

Westminster Abbey and Palace

To the west of the City, Westminster had no defensive walls and a much smaller population employed mainly in servicing the palace, abbey or the pilgrims who came to the shrine of St. Edward "the Confessor." The manor belonged to the abbey and it owned about two-thirds of the built-up area. In 1161 Edward the Confessor was canonized and his grave at the abbey became a popular pilgrimage center. In 1220 Henry III in an act of devotion to the Saint began the construction of a new Lady Chapel at the abbey. In 1245 he appointed the master mason Henry de Reyns to oversee the wholesale rebuilding of the church, which the king paid for at his own expense. Building was something of a sporadic affair, however, and it was only by 1532, the eve of the Protestant Reformation, that the last chantry chapel in the cathedral was finished and the nave completed to the design that Henry de Reyns

The Norman Cathedral of Westminster had been started in 1086 but this was substantially altered in the 13th century, including the addition of a spire in 1212. Between 1255 and 1283, the whole eastern end was rebuilt and extended in the Gothic style, with the addition of a rose window that was renowned for its exceptional beauty. Little survives of the original Norman church of Westminster Abbey, although the western end of the nave survived in this style. Pictured here is the Jewel Tower, built by Edward III around 1365 to house his personal treasures, with a moat dug around it for extra protection. It is virtually unaltered today, and is one of only two complete buildings remaining from the general complex of the medieval Palace of Westminster. In 1248 the cathedral was enclosed by a wall with six gates, and a two-story cloister and chapterhouse were added in the 1330s. In 1447 the spire was badly damaged by lightning and was not repaired for 15 years. Then in 1561 the whole structure burned down and was never replaced.

had begun nearly three hundred years before.

Next to the Abbey and structurally connected to it was the sprawling royal palace of Westminster. At the heart of the palace was the chapel of St. Stephen and William II's great hall. In 1298 Edward I began work on a new chapel, the previous one having been destroyed by fire a few years before. Edward's chapel was one of the first buildings in London to be built in the Perpendicular style. The chapel was not completed in Edward's lifetime but was finished by his grandson Edward III in 1347.

In 1393 Richard II began the complete rebuilding of William II's Hall at Westminster. Although Richard would never see the great hall finished—he was deposed in 1399—he was able to celebrate the Christmas of 1396 in the building when jousts were held down the length of the hall as part of the celebrations. Between the hall and the abbey were series of buildings, including the Exchequer chamber, around open courtyards. New Palace Yard ran down to the Thames where there was a watergate giving access from the river and where another building housed the Court of Star Chamber. Nearby stood the Parliament Chamber of the House of Lords.

Bridging the Thames

Southwark and London were linked by London Bridge. In 1176 the wooden bridge that had been built after the disastrous fire of 1136 was demolished and replaced by a stone bridge. To construct the

Heavily influenced by the French cathedrals of Rheims, Amiens and Sainte-Chapell in Paris, Westminster Abbey has been described as the most French of all the English Gothic churches. By 1254, the transepts, the north front, rose windows, chapter house and part of the cloister were all completed. In 1269 the choir was finished and work had advanced sufficiently on the nave for the body of St. Edward to be moved into a shrine in an especially dedicated chapel. Henry III—pictured holding a model of his new Abbey Church—died in 1272 and was buried in front of the altar in his rebuilt abbey, the first king to be buried there since 1066. Richard II contributed toward the costs of the rebuilding, but the cathedral did not receive regular financial support until the reign of Henry V (1413-22), also buried there). Edward IV, grateful to the abbey for giving his queen sanctuary in 1460, provided the funds for building a chapel. Between 1503 and 1519 Henry VII (1485-1509) replaced Henry III's Lady Chapel with one dedicated to the Virgin Mary, where in 1509 he was buried.

bridge 19 stone piers with wooden pile foundations were placed across the Thames. Each pier was protected from the flow of the river by a wooden boat-shaped structure called a "starling," these reduced the flow of the river drastically causing dangerous currents that easily could sink small boats. It was said that "London Bridge was built for wise men to go over and fools to go under."

In addition to the gate towers, there was a drawbridge—this could be raised for defense but also allowed ships to pass up and down the Thames. In

The wooden structure of the first London Bridge was renewed several times, and it was probably to this earliest bridge that the nursery rhyme "London Bridge is falling down" refers. It was eventually replaced with a 20-arch stone bridge in 1176. It took 30 years to complete, and houses and shops were incorporated to help pay for its upkeep.

the middle of the bridge was a chapel dedicated to St. Thomas à Becket. By 1201 the first houses were being built on the bridge and by 1460 the bridge had 129 houses on it. Because the bridge was so narrow, the houses were often built overhanging the sides and this could lead to accidents, as happened in 1481 when a house on the bridge collapsed into the river, drowning five men. Not for the last time, the bridge was seriously damaged by fire in 1212, and in 1282 five arches collapsed. Nevertheless it survived until it was replaced in 1831. The restriction of the river current by London Bridge caused the Thames to freeze over in cold winters, when Londoners would hold frost fairs on the ice.

The gate towers were not only used for defensive purposes: the heads of traitors would be displayed, after having been parboiled and dipped in tar, a tradition that started in 1305 with the head of the executed Scots leader William Wallace.

Suburbs and industry

In the areas surrounding London directly outside the walls, the city was beginning to acquire new suburbs. To the north beyond Moorgate, there were fields, gardens and marshes but to the east and west were suburbs. To the east around the Tower were armorers and braziers' workshops, and along the banks of the Thames the riverside villages were developing into areas where ships could be fitted out, repaired and provisioned. Inland away from the Thames there was industrial activity such as brickmaking, limeburning, metalwork and bellfounding, and further east along the banks of the River Lea were fulling mills. To the immediate west of London, the open ground between the City and Westminster was slowly being colonized.

The proximity of the palace had led to the building of many great houses along the Strand, and the courts at Westminster attracted lawyers to the area, which led to the foundation of the Inns of Court. By the late Middle Ages, the four Inns of

On the south side of the Thames, Southwark, like Westminster, preserved its independence from the city. Unlike Westminster however, Southwark was governed by five manorial courts and had a reputation for lawlessness. It was also famous for its prisons and the prostitutes who worked in brothels run by the Bishop of Winchester. Southwark was also a center of London's leather industry and the tanneries gave the air a foul smell. Despite this Southwark was on the main road to the channel ports and the pilgrim center of Canterbury. Southwark's high street was lined with inns where travelers and pilgrims would spend the night to avoid the city curfew and get an early start on their journey. This trade encouraged brewing, stabling and victualling which all provided good livelihoods for the area. The map shows a view from the Elizabethan period and which would have changed little from medieval times. Always noted for its inns— already made famous by Chaucer's Canterbury pilgrims—the area later became a focal point for theaters and bear-baiting pits.

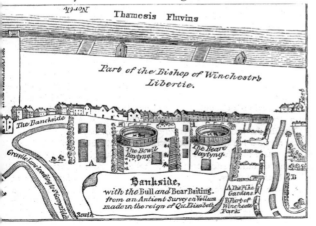

North

Thamesis Fluvius

Part of the Bishop of Winchestrs Libertie.

The Bankside

Gravile lane leading to Gunpole

The Bowll Baytyng. _The Beare Baytyng._

A

B

Bankside, with the Bull and Bear Baiting. from an Antient Survey on Vellum made in the reign of Qu.Elizabeth

A The Pike Gardens B Part of Winchester Park.

South

Court—Lincoln's Inn, Inner Temple, Middle Temple, and Grays Inn—were established as centers for the teaching and practice of the law.

Center of commerce

By the close of the Middle Ages, London had developed dramatically from the city that had surrendered to William the Conqueror in 1066. By 1400, London was one of the major trading ports of Western Europe and by far the greatest port in England. Wool and cloth were the nation's major exports and by the end of the 15th century, 45 percent of wool and 70 percent of the cloth exports were shipped via London. In return London imported wine from France as well as foodstuffs, manufactured items like weapons, armor, knives, linen, haberdashery and other textiles. There were luxury goods too: jewelry, glassware, soap, paper and books and even spectacles.

By the end of the 15th century, London had recovered from the ravages of the Black Death to become the largest city in England—it has been

The Corporation of London can trace its ancestry back to more than a thousand years and, after the monarchy, is the oldest secular institution in the country. From the reoccupation of London by Alfred the Great onwards, officials called "reeves" and a port-reeve (the title of a reeve of a town or trading place as opposed to a shire-reeve or sheriff who had a county responsibility) who, through assemblies of leading citizens and magistrates as well as the "folkmoot," governed the city. The folkmoot was an open-air council of all the citizens. Called three times a year, it may have met in the ruined Roman amphitheater. Some such continuity of use has been suggested because the medieval Guildhall (pictured), the administrative center of London, was later built on the amphitheater site. By the 13th century the folk-moot had moved to St. Paul's Cross, by St. Paul's Cathedral, and made decisions on matters such as guarding the city against fire and crime.

During the 11th century the "ward" system began to develop in London. Initially related to the defense of the city, the wards were responsible for maintaining the city walls and gates, and providing soldiers for defense. These were tax zones with responsibility for law and order, trade, and sanitation. The size of the wards depended on the number of people living there and the amount they were expected to contribute to the city's defense. "Aldermen" governed each ward, which had its own court, the "Wardmoot." The Wardmoot is still an integral part of the government of the City of London and meets every year. The Aldermen also have their own court, the "Court of Aldermen" which is first recorded in 1200. The Court of Aldermen along with the Court of Common Council still form the governing body of London, and are presided over by the "Lord Mayor", who is himself an Alderman elected by the Court of Aldermen at an electoral meeting called "Common Hall." Pictured is a 20th century gathering of "Ward Beadles" outside Guildhall during the election of City "Sheriffs."

estimated that one in forty of the national population lived there. Nevertheless it was still small by European standards—Paris, Brussels, Bruges and Ghent were all larger. What set London apart was that during the Middle Ages England had developed a strong centralized government based around the King, Parliament and the Law, with London and Westminster at its center as the undisputed political capital. Meanwhile, London's own government, the Corporation of London, whose position and independence was enshrined in successive charters, gradually evolved which, legally removed from excessive royal interference, gave London unrivaled political and economic stability.

Governing from the Guildhall

The building from which London is governed is the Guildhall, and the guilds of London form an important part in the history of the city and its administration. The first mention of a guildhall in London is in 1128, but in 1411 work began on a new building and the construction work would continue throughout the 15th century. On its completion the great hall (completed in 1430) was the largest in the country after the great hall of Westminster. Its size meant that in addition to its civic functions, such as housing the meetings of the Court of Common Council, the hall was used for important trials.

The guilds gain power

The London Guilds or City Livery Companies—from whom the Guildhall gets its name— originated

in the Middle Ages as trade organizations and fraternities. First mentioned in 1180, the aim of the guilds was to preserve and regulate craft skills, to promote trade (often meaning ensuring they held a monopoly in London), to regulate wages, working conditions and generally to look after the interests and welfare of their members. Guild members became known as "liverymen" because each guild had its own distinctive costume or livery. The guilds had considerable authority over their trades, with sweeping powers to inspect goods, confiscating those of poor standard or quality and punishing the workmen responsible.

The guilds conducted their business in halls they built in their trading

The Protestant preacher Anne Askew (see page 90) was tried in Westminster Hall for heresy in 1546. Others who faced trial there included the Earl of Surrey in 1547 for treason and Queen Jane and her husband Guildford Dudley in 1553. In the same year Thomas Cranmer, the Archbishop of Canterbury, was tried for heresy and in 1606 the Jesuit priest Henry Garnet was tried for his part in the Gunpowder Plot. The hall (left) was rebuilt with a double hammer beam roof, which was able to span the width of the hall without support. The new hall was one of the largest in the world without a supported roof. Below is a depiction of Garnet facing the crowd before his execution at Tyburn.

areas—so in Cordwainer Street could be found the shoemakers, the bakers were in Bread Street, tailors in Threadneedle Street. Other guilds were concentrated around Cheapside, the main marketplace for the city. Many of these halls were subsequently destroyed by the Great Fire of 1666 and rebuilt, or were re-sited in the 16th century on land taken from the church after the Reformation.

By the 14th century, the guilds were a powerful and wealthy force in the government of London and in 1376 they were given the sole right to elect the members of the Common Council, although this right was later extended to representatives from the wards. Nevertheless the guilds retained the right to elect the Lord Mayor and the Sheriff, and the guilds are still the sole electorate for these posts.

By the end of the Middle Ages, London was the undisputed principal city of the kingdom. England, unlike mainland Europe, had no tradition of city - states, and London—although sophisticated, wealthy and independent—still relied on the goodwill of the king. Nevertheless of all the cities of England, only London could and did challenge the government; yet it was its incorporation into the nation rather than separation from it that would prove of immense benefit to both kingdom and City in the centuries to come.

Admission to a guild was allowed to those who had served an appropriate apprenticeship. An apprentice would take seven years to learn his trade or craft and would then be admitted as a freeman to the guild. This meant that he was free to practice the skills he had learned. Workers without an apprenticeship were often included in the guilds as "yeomen." Other means of entering a guild were to be the son of a serving liveryman or through the payment of an entry fee. Relations between the various guilds were not always easy, and in the Middle Ages there were riots and battles in the city between competing guild members. By the end of the 14th century an "Order of Precedents" had been established for the various guilds. Today the guilds still exist though their number has increased from 12 original guilds to 94, and include companies as diverse as the Air Pilots' and Air Navigators' Guild (granted their livery in 1956), the Launderers' Company (1977), and the Scientific Instrument Makers' Company (1964). Pictured above left is the heading of a financial account showing a cooper at work, while below is a seal of the vintners' company.

CHAPTER 5
THE FLOWER OF CITIES ALL
TUDOR LONDON 1536-1603

"London, thou art of townes A per se. Sovereign of cities, semeliest in sight, Of high renoun, riches, and royaltie; Of lordis, barons, and many goodly knyght; Of most delectable lusty ladies bright; Of famous prelatis in habitis clericall; Of merchaunts full of substaunce and myght: London, thou art the flour of Cities all."

—William Dunbar,
To the City of London
(1501)

Although initially turbulent, the long reign of Queen Elizabeth I (pictured right) was marked as a Golden Age of peace and increased prosperity. This was particularly so for London, where the arts flourished and audiences flocked to public entertainments such as the scene from a play opposite, staged by actors at the Red Bull Playhouse.

I N 1483, EDWARD IV DIED, LEAVING his brother Richard Duke of Gloucester as protector for his two sons during their minority. The new king, Edward V, was only 13 years old and his brother only seven. The two princes were taken to the Tower of London and never seen again.

In the months that followed Richard purged his opponents and in July 1483 crowned himself as King Richard III (1483-1485) in Westminster Abbey. Despite the monarch's efforts to secure his throne, a claimant to the crown, Henry Tudor, the Duke of Richmond, had managed to escape to France. In 1485, Henry staked his claim to the throne by landing with his army in Wales, and he defeated Richard III in the Battle of Bosworth. Richard was killed and Henry was crowned Henry VII (1485-1509).

When the new king reached London he was greeted by the citizens at Shoreditch, there were trumpeters and he was presented with acclamations and loyal verses as well as a gift of money. The citizens who greeted Henry, at the gates of London could not have known that the accession of this king would bring to an end the civil wars that had plagued England throughout the 15th century, would establish a dynasty, the Tudors, who would occupy the throne for the next 118 years and would see the transition of England from a medieval kingdom to a modern state.

By the time Henry came to the throne the

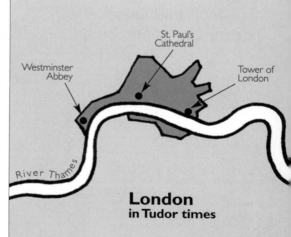

London
in Tudor times

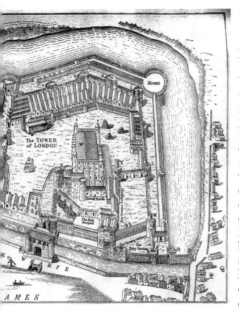

crown had changed hands five times in 30 years, and the new monarch was well aware of how precarious his position was. He proved a careful and astute ruler as well as a devout one who built chapels and convents. In London between 1300 and 1530 at least 50 parish churches were enlarged or rebuilt and 17 major new monastic houses were built. Bequests and gifts had made the church a wealthy London landowner; it has been estimated that by 1520 the church owned about two-thirds of the land in London.

Nevertheless Londoners were unafraid to challenge the church. In 1378 a mob had turned out to support the English heretic John Wycliffe. Wycliffe and his followers, known as Lollards, used a bible written in English, rejected the Pope, and opposed the worship of images or crosses. Although the Lollards enjoyed the sympathy of many Londoners, when in 1414 Sir John Oldcastle attempted to lead a Lollard rebellion against Henry V in London, the citizens offered him little support and the insurrection was easily put down. When Oldcastle was arrested he was executed in

King Henry VII's London subjects were proud of their own London-born saint, Thomas à Becket, the Archbishop of Canterbury (martyred in 1170). London had two local pilgrim attractions. In Bermondsey Abbey, just across the Thames from the city, pilgrims would come to see the "Rood of Grace," an Anglo-Saxon cross which had been found in the Thames but was thought to have dropped from heaven and to have miraculous power. To the west, in Westminster Abbey, stood the magnificent shrine of St. Edward the Confessor.

Above left: A view of the Tower of London and its surrounding moat from a survey made in 1597.

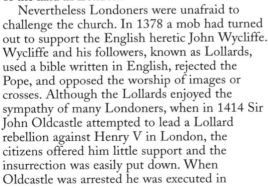

London without incident.

Nevertheless by the 1520s Lollardy was enjoying something of a revival in London. As the largest city in the kingdom, London's size allowed Protestants like the Lollards to act in relative anonymity. This, combined with frequent contact with merchants from Germany and the Low Countries, provided a fertile bed for the ideas of the Protestant reformist Martin Luther, which had begun to circulate in the city by 1518, and by 1526 the first editions of Tindale's English translation of the New Testament could be found in the city.

Henry VIII (1509-47) inherited the crown of England at the age of 17. Unusually for a monarch, he was extremely well-educated and cultured—he sponsored the arts, played and composed music (and wrote the lyrics to "Greensleeves"), spoke several languages and wrote theological essays. Very much a Renaissance man, he was also a fanatical sportsman and jouster. Before he was excommunicated for replacing the Pope with himself as the head of the Church of England, the Pope awarded him the title "Defender of the Faith" for writing a treatise denouncing Martin Luther's Reformist ideals against Rome.

Healthy anti-clericalism

While the majority of Londoners may not have been Lollards or Protestants, most seem to have enjoyed a healthy, though not overt anti-clericalism. Chaucer had mocked the clergy in his *Canterbury Tales* (written in the 1380s) and in 1468 when the cordwainers (leatherworkers) were ordered by a Papal Bull to close their shops on Sundays some responded by declaring that "the Pope's curse is not worth a fly!"

The capital's priests, monks and friars were widely regarded as drunken and debauched, although in reality this was rare. Only one or two clerics were ever brought to trial each year, but this was enough, as Henry's Lord Chancellor Thomas More explained: "Let a lewd Friar be taken with a wench, we will jest and rail upon the whole order all the year after, and say Lo what an example they gave us!"

In 1511, John Colet, Dean of St. Paul's, gave voice to these attitudes in a sermon where he attacked the clergy claiming "they give themselves to feasts and banqueting; they spend themselves in vain babbling; they give themselves to sports and plays; they apply themselves to hunting and hawking; they drown themselves in the delights of this world."

More's predecessor Thomas Wolsey personified this attitude. As well as that of Lord Chancellor, Wolsey also held the titles of Cardinal and Archbishop of York (a city he never visited) and so was the highest-ranking English churchman. But he was an unpopular minister and his less than spiritual lifestyle encouraged his opponents, particularly since he had two illegitimate sons. He was fantastically rich and lived

Henry played on the perceived excesses of the clergy (such as the drinking monk, right) to seize their possessions and destroy their buildings. The gateway below, built in 1504, has survived as part of the 12th-century Priory of St. John of Jerusalem, Clerkenwell.

in luxury in York Place, his palace in London, or at his palace of Hampton Court, where he had over 400 servants all dressed in richly embroidered livery.

Pursuing the heretics

By the 1520s, Cuthbert Tunstall, the Bishop of Durham, had unearthed more heretics in London than were found almost anywhere else in the country, and it was from London that Thomas More directed

his persecution of heretics between 1529 and 1532. He pursued dissident pamphleteers, publishers and book agents, imprisoning them in the Tower or in his own house in Chelsea. Not only did he burn heretical books, he also had their authors burned at the stake.

However, by 1527 Henry VIII had fallen in love with Anne Boleyn, the daughter of one of his courtiers. The king had been considering divorce from his wife, Katherine of Aragon, for some time but now his mind was made up. Wolsey was ordered to obtain a divorce from the pope and in 1529 the matter was sent to Rome. Pope Clement VII would not grant a divorce. Enraged, Henry dismissed Wolsey and had him charged with treason. The king meanwhile was

Anti-clerical sentiments were further enraged in 1514 when Richard Hunne was found hanged in his cell while awaiting trial in the Bishop of London's prison in the grounds of St. Paul's. Hunne was a London citizen and respected member of the guild of Merchant Taylors who had been involved in a dispute with the rector of Whitechapel over fees for the funeral of his baby son. Hunne had had Lollard sympathies so the Bishop had his body burned as that of a heretic, a charge that deprived his family of any inheritance they might have enjoyed. There was widespread sympathy for Hunne throughout London and a coroner's jury found that the Bishop's gaoler had murdered him. But the Bishop claimed it would be impossible to find a jury in London willing to acquit his servant. Pictured is the chamber in Lambeth Palace in which those charged with being Lollards were imprisoned.

determined to get his divorce by other methods.

In November 1529, Henry summoned a parliament—known as the Reformation Parliament—to discuss the matter; he hoped that by doing this he would put pressure on the Church. In its first year, the parliament protested about churchmen who held secular offices, pluralism and the non-residence of churchmen. The following year the entire English clergy was charged under the "Statute of Praemunire," i.e. that they usurped the King's authority by obtaining judgments from the Pope. The Church did not oppose Henry and instead paid him £118,000 in fines.

Nevertheless Henry's attempt to pressure Rome through Parliament failed, and between 1532 and 1535 Parliament enacted a series of statutes that removed the Pope's authority over the church. The Archbishop of Canterbury authorized Henry's divorce and in 1534 the Act of Succession gave the throne to any children born from the union between Anne Boleyn and Henry, thus excluding his daughter Mary (from his marriage to Katherine). The Act of Supremacy was then passed, declaring the King to be the supreme head of the Church in England. Failure

Pope Clement VII first praised Henry VIII for his spirited defence of Catholicism against Martin Luther and the Reformation, but was forced to excommunicate him when the monarch made himself the supreme head of the Church of England. Below is the marriage procession of Henry VIII's second wife Anne Boleyn through the streets of London.

by anyone to swear an oath of allegiance to these two acts was declared treasonous by the Treason Act.

What Londoners thought of these changes is not known, but it was unwise to speak out against them, as those who did risked arrest and execution. The majority seem to have quietly accepted the changes. When in 1534 the people were required to swear the Oath of Succession, only Thomas More, now retired as the

Thomas More (1478-1535)—the Man for All Seasons—rose from humble origins to become an accomplished judge and diplomat, finally becoming Lord Chancellor under Henry VIII. He also had a reputation throughout Europe as a humanist writer and thinker whose most famous work was "Utopia". Moore's principles led him to refuse to acknowledge Henry as the Head of the Church of England and he was excuted at the Tower. He was made a saint in 1935.

Bishop of Rochester, and a single London priest refused and were executed. Even Bishop Tunstall, who previously had eagerly persecuted any form of deviation from the Church, took the oath.

Dissolution of the monasteries

Henry now turned his attention toward the monasteries. In 1532, the prior of Holy Trinity Aldgate, faced with heavy debts, had been forced to surrender his priory to the Crown along with land valued at £300 in various London parishes. Although this was one of London's most famous monasteries, the citizens showed no interest in protecting it. Henry now embarked on the Dissolution of the Monasteries and the seizure of their assets. One of his first targets was the order of Franciscan Friars Observant adjacent to his palaces at Richmond and Greenwich. The friars were critical of Henry's marriage to Anne Boleyn and refused to acknowledge the king's spiritual authority. Henry acted and the

entire order in England was suppressed in 1534, and some 200 friars were imprisoned.

In 1536 an Act of Parliament dissolved all the monasteries worth £200 or less—of the 350 houses that closed, only one, St. Mary Spittal, was in London, and it was closed without any objection from Londoners. Over the following three years, the king's principal secretary Thomas Cromwell acting under the title of Vicar General tried to pressure the large monastic houses into voluntary surrender in return for generous pensions and church offices elsewhere. Charterhouse, whose monks had suffered death in their opposition to Henry's divorce, closed voluntarily in 1537.

Those monasteries that did not agree to go were forced in 1539 when an Act of Parliament extended monastic closure to those houses with a value of over

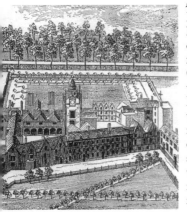

£200. Within four years London's monasteries had almost all gone—the only comment coming from Sir Richard Gresham, who asked that the Corporation of London be allowed to take over some of the monastic hospitals in order to stop the spread of disease and that some of the monastic churches remain open for worship

When the Act of Supremacy was passed in 1535, three Carthusian monks from London led by John Houghton, the prior of Charterhouse (pictured in bird's-eye view below left), argued against it. They were sent to the Tower of London and charged with treason, where another London monk joined them. On May 4, 1535, they were executed as traitors. This involved being dragged through the streets on hurdles (wooden frames) to Tyburn where they were hanged and while still alive taken down and cut into quarters. More of the monks from Charterhouse suffered the same fate. Some were arrested and sent to the prison of Newgate where they were chained upright, some dying of starvation before they could be executed.

Some monasteries did manage to survive the Dissolution in an altered form. St. Katherine's by the Tower, traditionally under the patronage of the Queen, was saved at the request of Anne Boleyn and is still in existence. Westminster Abbey with its royal connections and mausoleums survived, but under a bishop. The abbey did lose much of its land, some being taken by the crown, and some being given to St Paul's in the City, giving rise to the proverb "robbing Peter to pay Paul"—Westminster Abbey being dedicated to St. Peter. Several monasteries survived as hospitals, including St. Bartholomew's (pictured today, left, with a staue of King Hreny VIII), St Thomas's, and Bethlehem, better known as Bedlam.

"by reason of the great multitude of people daily resorting to parish churches to the annoyance of parishioners." His petition was not granted. Henry benefited greatly from the dissolution—it has been estimated that from the London monasteries alone he raised £70,000, this at a time when the normal annual Crown revenue was about £100,000.

Changes in the Church

The Reformation brought other changes too, especially to the traditional church festivals and celebrations. One of the most popular of these celebrations was the Midsummer Watch, a vigil that ushered in the longest day of the feast of St. John the Baptist. John Stow described these vigils in his *Survey of London*, written in 1598: "There were usually made bonfires in the streets, every man bestowing wood or labor toward them: the wealthier sort also before their doors near to the said bonfires, would set out tables, furnished with sweet bread and good drink, whereunto they would invite their neighbors, every man's door being shadowed with green birch, long fennel, St. John's wort, orpin, white lilies and such like garnished upon with garlands of beautiful flowers, had also lamps of glass with oil burning in them all the night."

Despite the changes in the Church, Henry VIII was not a Protestant—in fact, in 1539 he had expressed his liking for elements of the old religion such as Candlemas candles, Ash Wednesday ashes, Palm Sunday "palms" and the tradition of Creeping to the Cross at Easter, whereby the clergy present at the ceremony would crawl on their hands and knees without their shoes to a crucifix by the altar and kiss it while hymns were sung. In 1540, the king called for particular care to be taken during the Rogation processions, where fields were blessed for the forthcoming harvest with banners, crosses and holy water. This was despite the Protestant condemnation that they were "uplandish processions and gangings about which be spent in rioting and in belchery."

So in 1540, when the Vicar General Thomas Cromwell fell from favor and was executed, the Protestants lost their most influential supporter and their persecution

The Midsummer Watch was especially spectacular in 1521 thanks to a generous donation from the Draper's Guild. The Watch included floats and pageants representing the Castle of War, the Story of Jesse, St John the Evangelist, St. George and Pluto who was accompanied by a serpent which spat fireballs. In addition there was a model giant called "Lord Marlinspikes," morris dancers, naked boys dyed black to represent devils, armoured halberdiers, and a "King of the Moors" in satin robes, silver shoes and a turban crowned with white feathers. In 1539, with the Reformation at its height, the Government banned London's Midsummer Watch. Its motive was more political than religious. The problem with the Watch was that such a large and boisterous gathering celebrating the old religion could easily turn to riot or rebellion. The following year the Watch was replaced by a pageant of floats depicting Bible stories before the inauguration of the Lord Mayor. In the form of the Lord Mayor's Show, this is still celebrated today and was intended to be a safe and purely civic celebration.

resumed. Three Protestant London preachers were burned at Smithfield within a week of Cromwell's death. Protestant preachers were forced to recant publicly at St. Paul's Cross and in 1546 Anne Askew was arrested for preaching to London laborers. The arrest and torture in the Tower of London of Askew, who was only 25 years old, was immortalized by John Fox in his *Book of Martyrs*, Fox recounts that "first, she was led down into a dungeon, where Sir Anthony Knevet, the lieutenant, commanded his gaoler to pinch her with the rack... and so quietly and patiently praying unto the Lord, she abode their tyranny, till her bones and joints were almost plucked asunder, so

A contemporary print recording "The Manner of Burning Anne Askew, John Lacels, John Adams, and Nicolas Belenian, with Certane of ye Counsell sitting in Smithfield." Such public spectacles of executing Catholics or Protestants were less concerned with faith than with making a highly visible political example of how the English state viewed internal dissent.

that she was carried away in a chair." Askew would not recant and was executed by burning at Smithfield; again Fox describes the scene: "The day of her execution being appointed, she was brought to Smithfield in a chair, because she could not walk, from the cruel effects of the torments. When she was brought to the stake, she was fastened to it by the middle with a chain that held up her body. Three others were brought to suffer with her... The martyrs being chained to the stake, and all things ready for the fire... The sermon being finished, the martyrs, standing at three several stakes ready to their martyrdom, began their prayers. The multitude of the people was exceeding great, the place where they stood being railed about to keep out the press. Upon the bench, under St. Bartholomew's church, sat Wriothesley, the Chancellor of England, the old Duke of Norfolk, the old Earl of Bedford, the Lord Mayor, with divers others. Before the fire was kindled, one of the bench hearing that they had gunpowder about them, and being afraid lest the fagots, by strength of the gunpowder, would come flying about their ears, began to be afraid; but the gunpowder was not laid under the faggots, but only about their bodies to rid them of their pain."

Destroying the Old Church

In 1547 Henry VIII died and was succeeded by his nine-year-old son Edward VI, whose reign ushered in a period of staunchly Protestant government. Under Edward VI many of the old traditions and methods of worship were outlawed. In September 1547 most of the images in St. Paul's Cathedral were destroyed and two months later the remainder were pulled down, although this was done at night because the reformers feared that there might be opposition.

Within 18 months of his accession, Edward's government had destroyed the remaining festivals, images and institutions of the Old Church. London offered no resistance to the changes—not even when

By the beginning of 1548 all images had been removed from the churches of London. Royal proclamation forbade the traditions of Candlemas, Ash Wednesday, Palm Sunday and "Creeping to the Cross" at Easter. The same year the parishes of London and Westminster abandoned the tradition of keeping vigil at an Easter sepulcher. This had originally been done in commemoration of the soldiers who guarded Christ's Tomb. The Rogation procession was ended in London and the crosses where the procession had stopped were "thrown down."

in 1549 a Protestant preacher denounced the Cornhill
Maypole as idolatrous and it was chopped up and
burned. This maypole, which was taller than the
nearby steeple of St. Andrew's Church, had been set
up annually for the Mayday celebrations. However it
had not been used since 1517 when the Mayday
celebrations had ended in riots.

Bells ring for Mary

In 1553 at the age of 16, Edward VI died. Despite an
unsuccessful attempt by the Duke of Northumberland to install the Protestant Lady Jane Grey on the
throne, Edward was succeeded by his Catholic half-
sister Mary. To the population it was obvious that
Mary was the rightful heir and she was welcomed in
London. One contemporary observer wrote of the
celebrations: "I saw myself money was thrown out at
windows for joy. The bonfires were without number,
and what with the shouting, and crying of the people,
and the ringing of bells there could be no man hear
what another
said."

The good
relationship
that Mary had
with her
subjects was
not to last; in
part this was
because of the
queen's
determination
to marry the
king of Spain,
Philip I. In
January 1554,
Sir Thomas
Wyatt raised a
rebellion in
Kent over the

One tradition that did
not receive royal
displeasure was the Lord
of Misrule, who presided
over the Christmas
celebrations. The monarch's
Lord of Misrule developed
a tradition of making a
state entry into London
accompanied by
bagpipers, morris
dancers and gaolers
who carried with them
instruments of punish-
ment. The Sheriff of
London's Lord of Misrule,
also accompanied by a
retinue, would then
greet them and they
would ride through the
City. Another key festival
in the calendar, eventually
banned, was the dancing
around the Maypole
(below).

issue of the queen's marriage. Londoners were sympathetic to Wyatt but by the time his army had arrived at the gates of London Bridge, the queen had made a direct appeal to the citizens of London and had declared Wyatt a traitor. The result was that he found London Bridge closed to him. The rebel leader was taken to the

Tower and executed along with the hapless Lady Jane Grey.

Despite Wyatt's rebellion, the queen continued with her plan to marry Philip of Spain and embarked on a policy of reconciliation with the Church of Rome. Protestants were once again persecuted after 1554 and by the end of Mary's reign 270 Protestants were executed—43 of the executions took place in Smithfield in London. Although this was a relatively small number, the political effect on Mary's cause proved catastrophic. The persecution of Protestants was seen as Spanish-driven, and the result was that Protestantism swiftly became viewed as a purely English religion while Catholicism became associated with foreign oppression. The executed Protestants accordingly became English martyrs.

Ascendancy of the Virgin Queen

Mary died childless in 1558 and the throne passed to her half-sister Elizabeth, the "Virgin Queen." Elizabeth was to rule for the next 45 years, one of the longest reigns in English history. Under her rule the Protestant church and Royal supremacy were restored, although many of the old religious wounds were healed.

Although the Tudor monarchs were responsible for the loss of London's monastic houses, they were also responsible for giving the city its greatest palaces. In

Relations with Spain, at the time the greatest power in Europe, deteriorated and in the summer of 1588, the king of Spain sent against England the invasion force known today as the Armada. Arrangements were made to defend London—a boom was stretched across the Thames at Tilbury to prevent ships from getting upstream and also to act as a bridge to allow the English army to cross the river. Cannon were placed on each bend in the river, and London alone managed to raise an irregular force of 10,000 armed men. In the event, none of these defenses were necessary and the Armada was defeated at sea. To celebrate, fires were lit across the country and Queen Elizabeth held a tournament at St. James's Palace. The captured ensigns from Spanish ships were displayed in London.

addition to their palaces at Westminster and the Tower of London, the English monarchs had always had smaller palaces and hunting lodges scattered around the city, such as Kennington in south London where the Black Prince, the son of Edward III had his palace. At Eltham, also in the south of London, there was a magnificent palace with the third greatest hall in the kingdom where every English monarch from Henry III to Henry VIII traditionally would go to celebrate Christmas.

Under Henry VIII, the monarchy obtained its most splendid London palaces. In a vain attempt to regain the king's favor and retain his position at court, Cardinal Wolsey had presented Henry VIII with his own palace at Hampton Court. Henry set about enlarging and adding to Wolsey's original building and created a magnificent garden and a well-stocked game park for hunting. It was in the chapel of Hampton Court that Jane Seymour married Henry VIII the day after the execution of Anne Boleyn, and it was in the palace that she died after bearing Henry's only legitimate son, Edward VI. It

Henry VII built the magnificent palace of Richmond, covering over ten acres at Sheene. Henry VIII spent his childhood in the palace. Queen Mary I and Philip II of Spain chose it for their honeymoon in 1554, and Queen Elizabeth I died there in 1603. Charles I (1626-1649) added to the palace when he created Richmond Park, enclosed within a ten-mile brick wall. The 2,250-acre park was a hunting ground for deer. After the English Civil War (1642-1649), the palace lost its appeal and sank into disuse—its contents were sold off, and by the end of the 17th century it had been demolished.

was also here that Catherine Howard begged in vain for her life as Henry heard mass in the chapel.

His daughter Elizabeth I staged spectacular banquets at Hampton Court as well as staging plays in the great hall. Charles I was held a prisoner at the palace after the Civil War, and during the Republic that followed his death it was used by the dictator Oliver Cromwell (1653-1658) as a residence—and it was subsequently occupied by every monarch until the reign of George II (1727-1760). In 1851, Queen Victoria presented the palace to the nation.

Cardinal Wolsey's fall from grace also allowed Henry to take over York Place, the London residence of the Archbishops of York, situated between the City and Westminster. The king renamed it Whitehall and set about a major rebuilding campaign. He built cockpits, tennis courts and a tiltyard where tournaments were held. Inhabitants of the palace were instructed to be "loving together, of good unity and accord" and were to ensure that they were not "grudging or rumbling or talking of the King's pastime." This palace would eclipse the ancient palace at Westminster, which now became almost exclusively the home of Parliament. It was at Whitehall that Henry VIII died in 1547.

Between 1532 and 1540, Henry had already built a new palace on the site of the dissolved hospital of St. James to the west of Westminster, which he called St.

Situated at a great bend in the river Thames below the City, Greenwich was the favorite palace of Henry VIII and Elizabeth I, both of whom were born there, as was Queen Mary I. It was at the Mayday celebrations at Greenwich in 1536 that Henry's second wife, Anne Boleyn, was accused of dropping her handkerchief as a signal to her lover, and where Henry signed the order for her execution. Like Richmond further upstream, the palace suffered during the English Republic (1649-60) when it was used to house Dutch prisoners of war. Despite this, Charles II began work on a new palace, which was never completed and was abandoned during the reign of William and Mary (1689-1695).

Both James I and
Charles I were residents
of Whitehall (left) and it
was outside the Banque-
ting Hall (built in the
palace by his father) that
Charles I was executed.
Oliver Cromwell used
Whitehall as an official
residence while he was
Lord Protector, and it was
here that he died in 1658.
William III did not like
the "air" around White-
hall as he suffered from
asthma, so he and Mary
II moved out to Kensing-
ton Palace, then in 1698
the old palace was
destroyed by fire. Below,
great houses on the old
London Bridge.

James's Palace. Attached to his new palace was a park, some of which survives today as St. James's Park, the oldest of London's royal parks. Queen Mary I died in the palace and it was here that Charles I spent the night before his execution. Following the destruction of Whitehall by fire in 1698 it became the principal royal residence in London. Queen Anne (1702-1714) established her court at the palace and it has remained the official residence of the monarch (though since 1837 the monarch actually has lived in Buckingham Palace). Foreign ambassadors are still accredited as being "ambassadors to the Court of St. James."

"Nonesuch" House

Henry VIII had one more significant palace in the vicinity of London. In 1538, he began work a few miles to the southwest of London on the site of the village of Cuddington, which the king cleared to build a great house. The new palace was built using materials from the dissolved priory at Merton, and was named "Nonesuch" as Henry was

determined that there would be no other building like it.

Using a 500-strong workforce—many of them Italians—Henry erected a sumptuously decorated two-story Renaissance palace around two interconnected courtyards. On the south front there were two decorated towers topped with domes. The whole edifice was set in a lavish park with gardens, fountains, sculptures and a maze. Spectacular though the house and gardens were, in 1556 Mary I exchanged it with the Earl of Arundel for lands in Suffolk, although it passed back into royal hands under Elizabeth I and was used as a hunting lodge by James I and his son Charles I. Following the end of the English Republic it was restored to the monarchy but was given by Charles II to his mistress, who subsequently sold it in 1682. Following the sale, the building was demolished.

It was not, however, just the monarch who was building new palaces in and around London. As a result of the Reformation, much land and the palaces that had once belonged to the Church fell into the hands of courtiers and merchants. Many of these palaces were centered on the Strand, the road that links the City to Westminster. The Duke of Somerset, while Protector to the young Edward VI,

It was at the palace of Durham House that a servant, on seeing Sir Walter Raleigh smoking tobacco and believing that he was on fire, attempted to douse him with a mug of ale.

Below is pictured the front of Raleigh's private house.

had built the magnificent palace of Somerset House on land that had formerly belonged to the church, using stone from demolished churches and monastic buildings.

The play's the thing!

However it is not for its palaces that Tudor London is best remembered—instead it is for the rise of the Elizabethan theater and as a golden age for playwrights such as Ben Johnson (1572-1637), Christopher Marlow (1564-1593) and most famously William Shakespeare (1564-1616). Since the Middle Ages, plays had been performed in London wherever they could get an audience, usually in the yards of the inns. However

continued restrictions imposed by the Corporation of London made the performance of plays increasingly difficult. In 1576, the carpenter and actor James

Burbage built "The Theatre," London's first playhouse in Shoreditch, which was outside the City's jurisdiction yet close enough for Londoners to walk to. Other theaters quickly followed: a year after Burbage

Elizabethan theaters such as The Swan (above) and The Globe (left) were circular or sub-circular buildings with three tiers of galleries facing the stage around an unroofed courtyard. The courtyard effectively was a standing area from which the performances could be watched. The larger theaters could accommodate up to 3,000 people, but plays were relatively expensive. In the 1590s it would cost a penny to stand and watch a play from the courtyard, approximately a fifth of a laborer's daily wage.

opened The Theatre, Henry Lanman built The Curtain virtually next-door to it.

But it was among the bear pits and brothels of Bankside, safe from the interference of the City authorities on the south banks of the Thames, that the real Elizabethan theater would take root. The Rose theater of 1587 was the first to be built, followed by The Swan in 1594-6. In 1597 James Burbage died, and the following year the lease on The Theatre at Shoreditch expired, so his two sons Cuthbert and Richard demolished the old playhouse and reused the materials to create a new theater across the Thames in Bankside, which they named The Globe.

The City authorities continually attempted to close the theaters; the Lord Mayor of London complained in a letter to the Privy Council that the theaters "give opportunity to the refuse sort of evil-disposed and ungodly people that are within and about this city to assemble themselves... they are the ordinary places for vagrant persons, masterless men, thieves, horse-stealers, whoremongers, cozeners, coney-catchers, contrivers of treason, and other idle and dangerous persons to meet together... they maintain idleness in such persons who have no vocation, and draw apprentices and other servants from their ordinary work."

The number of theaters in Bankside and a positive shift in attitude toward plays and performers under Elizabeth's successor, James I, led to the closure of many of the Bankside theaters and the opening instead of smaller establishments to the north of the Thames. The Swan rarely showed a play after 1601 and is not

The hostility of the City authorities to actors led performing companies to seek the protection of powerful men. The two most important of these Elizabethan troupes were The Lord Admiral's Men under the patronage of Lord Howard, the Admiral of the Fleet, and The Lord Chamberlain's Men, who enjoyed the patronage of Lord Hunsdon, the Lord Chamberlain. The Lord Admiral's Men were closely associated with Christopher Marlow and performed at the Rose Theatre and the Fortune. The Lord Chamberlain's Men included William Shakespeare (pictured) and performed at the Globe and at Blackfriars.

recorded after 1632. The Rose was demolished in 1606 and its owners moved their acting company to the Fortune. They also built the Hope in Bankside in 1614, but this was a combined theater and bear garden that after 1616 concentrated on animal baiting.

The City talks shop

The Tudor period also saw a massive rise in London's commerce. Lombard Street had traditionally been the meeting place for merchants wishing to conduct business. Stow describes how merchants would meet there twice a day but that the meetings were often "unpleasant and troublesome, by reason of walking and talking in an open street, being there constrained to endure all extremes of weather, or else to shelter themselves in shops."

From the beginning of the 16th century there had been various attempts to build a covered exchange building, but it was not till the 1560s that Thomas Gresham, formerly the Crown Agent in Antwerp, used a portion of his personal fortune to build the Royal Exchange on land purchased by the City.

Under James, the Crown was also prepared to directly patronize the theater. In 1603, the king granted letters patent to The Lord Chamberlain's Men who were renamed The King's Men, and another troupe The Queen's Men were formed under the patronage of James's wife Queen Anne. The King's Men performed at the Globe in the summer and at Blackfriars in the winter. The Queen's Men, under the direction of Christopher Beeston, initially performed at the Curtain before moving to the Red Bull in Clarkenwell and later the Cockpit in Drury Lane, as well as the playhouse at Salisbury Court and the nearby Whitefriars Playhouse.

Anxious to create a modern business forum, Gresham laid the first brick in June 1566 and the building took only 17 months to complete. Based on the Bourses in Antwerp and Venice it comprised of a two-story colon-naded arcade around a central piazza; above this were two floors of offices and shops. The building incorporated a large column with a bell to summon the merchants topped by a golden grasshopper, Gresham's emblem. Initially merchants were slow to take advantage of the exchange and Gresham had to offer free rent to those who would stock and light the shops. By 1570, the ex-change was thriving and in that year following a visit from Queen Elizabeth I it was renamed the Royal Exchange.

The presence of the Royal Exchange in London stimulated the formation of syndicates of merchants who funded voyages of exploration in return for charters granting mono-polistic trading rights. These voyages were made easier by the growth of wharves and shipyards along the River Thames. On the north bank, there was Wapping which began to develop as a village inextricably linked to shipping. Adjacent to Wapping was Ratcliffe, where warships had been built during the Hundred Years War (1339-1453). The village there had become increasingly orientated toward shipbuilding. Then there was Blackwall, well suited to larger vessels, with docks that were begun in the 16th century and became associated with the shipping needs of the East India Company.

On the south bank of the Thames was Rotherhithe, a small fishing village where the fleet of Edward the

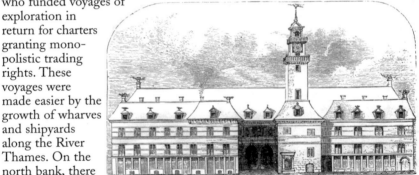

The sign of the Grasshopper (which has topped both the subsequent Exchanges) became a symbol of trade at the exchange so when in 1740 Peter Faneuil built Faneuil Hall in Boston, Massachusetts, he topped his market hall with a golden grasshopper. Gresham's Royal Exchange (pictured, its tower topped by the grasshopper) stood for a hundred years before the Great Fire of London destroyed it. It was replaced by another Exchange building built to the same pattern, this stood till 1838 when it too was destroyed by fire. The present Royal Exchange dates from this period.

"Black Prince" had been fitted out during the Hundred Years War and which was now developing into a growing port. Further downriver was Deptford where Henry VIII had created his world-renowned Royal Dockyard in 1513.

Adventurers and explorers

This, then, was a golden age of English exploration, funded by the wealth of London's merchants. These Elizabethan explorers included Sir Hugh Willoughby who sailed from London in 1553 with three ships in search of a northeast passage to China and the East Indies. Willoughby's ship was lost in Lapland but his pilot Richard Chancellor survived the winter on the Arctic White Sea and eventually reached Moscow where he negotiated favorable trading terms with the Tsar, and based on these negotiations the Muscovay Company was founded in 1555.

Between 1557 and 1560, Anthony Jenkinson opened a new route from the White Sea through Russia and the Caspian to the Central Asian trade center of Bukhara, diverting priceless trade from the old Silk Route. Between 1576 and 1578 Martin Frobisher, who had already explored the African coast, led several expeditions in search of the northwest passage to China. He reached Labrador, Baffin Island and Frobisher Bay, which is named after him. In 1610, Henry Hudson followed his route and gave his name to the Hudson Straits before sailing up the Hudson River.

These expeditions led to the formation of colonies and trading links throughout the world. Frobisher had attempted to found colonies in Canada and Sir Walter Raleigh had tried to establish a colony he called "Virginia," near Roanoke in modern-day North Carolina, before his 1596 expedition up the Orinoco River in modern-day Venezuela in search of the treasure of Eldorado. These early attempts to colonize America failed, and it was not till 1606 that Captain John Smith set sail from London to found the first permanent English colony in America at Jamestown, Virginia.

The chartered companies created by this exploration were vital for England's relations and trade and subsequent imperial development. Those companies that traded with the Old World maintained English influence overseas. But it was the companies who traded with the Indies and the New World that would be responsible for generating the vast wealth as well as colonies that would found the British Empire. Companies such as the East India Company (1600) and in North America the London Company or Virginia Company of London (1606), the Plymouth Company (1606) and the Massachusetts Bay Company (1629) all directly encouraged and founded colonies. The Hudson Bay Company (1670) was the exception, being almost solely concerned with trade.

End of a dynasty

The Tudor period came to an end at Richmond Palace in 1603 when Elizabeth died after 44 years on the throne. The queen's body was placed in a lead coffin and sailed up the river to Whitehall Palace to lie in state. At the funeral, an effigy of the queen, dressed in the robes of state with a crown and scepter, was laid on her coffin draped with purple velvet and covered by a canopy held by six knights.

The funeral carriage was drawn from the palace at Whitehall to Westminster Abbey by four horses draped in black. Elizabeth's own horse, riderless, followed behind. Then came the mourners led by the Marchioness of Northampton, followed by 266 poor women.

John Stow watched the funeral and wrote: "Westminster was surcharged with multitudes of all sorts of people that came to see. There was such a general sighing, groaning and weeping as the like hath not been seen or known in the memory of man, neither doth any history mention any people, time or state to make like lamentation for the death of their sovereign."

At Westminster Abbey, the Queen was interred alongside her half-sister Mary. With Elizabeth's death the great Tudor dynasty founded by Henry VII in 1485 came to an end. During that time England had changed from a medieval kingdom to a modern state and nascent imperial power.

It was at Deptford, in 1581, that Francis Drake and his crew made their first landfall after a two-year circumnavigation of the globe. Drake, only the second man to achieve this feat, was the first Englishman ever to do so. The expedition had been financed by a syndicate of London merchants. Drake returned laden with plunder from the Spanish Empire of South America, Queen Elizabeth met him at Deptford, dined with him and knighted him on board his ship, the Golden Hinde (pictured opposite).

CHAPTER 6
REBELLION AND RESTORATION
STUART LONDON 1603-1702

"Behold now this vast city, a city of refuge, the mansion-house of liberty, encompassed and surrounded with his protection; the shop of war hath not there more anvils and hammers waking to fashion out the plates and instruments of armed justice in defense of beleaguered truth, than there be pens and heads there, sitting by their studious lamps, musing, searching, revolving new notions and ideas wherewith to present, as with their homage and their fealty — others as fast reading, trying all things, assenting to the force of reason and convincement. What could a man require more from a nation so pliant and so prone to seek after knowledge?"
—John Milton, *Areopagatica* (1644)

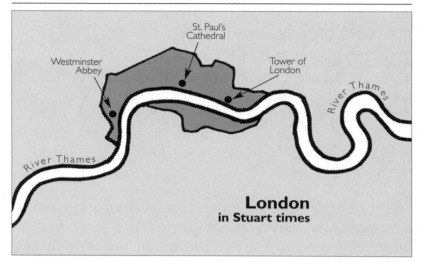

St. Paul's
Cathedral

Westminster
Abbey

Tower of
London

River Thames

River Thames

London
in Stuart times

LIZABETH NEVER MARRIED AND
when she died she had no direct heir.
Instead the throne passed to King James VI
of Scotland, who became James I of
England (1604-1625), the first king of the
House of Stuart. The new monarch arrived in
London to take his throne during an outbreak of
plague, which killed an estimated 30,000 Londoners,
and his coronation was therefore postponed. In
accordance with tradition, the king spent the night
before the ceremony at the Tower of London (the last
monarch ever to do so). The next day, the route
between the Tower and Westminster was thronged
with crowds; there was pageantry and music as well
as a series of triumphal arches to welcome the new
king. It took the royal party six hours to cover the
few miles to Westminster Abbey.

   The outbreak of plague that had delayed
James's coronation was a reminder that
London's large population was at constant
risk from disease. The authorities also feared

Previous page: The
lavish interior of the
Banqueting House on
Whitehall, outside which
Charles I, pictured on
horseback, was
beheaded by the
Republicans.
Below: Charles' father,
the Scot
James I.

that such a large concentration of people might lead to difficulties in maintaining law and order, especially if there were problems with food supplies during bad harvests. And so, from the 1580s onward, various attempts were made to restrict or control the city's apparently unstoppable expansion; the population of London grew from about 75,000 in 1550 to 200,000 by 1600 and up to 400,000 by 1640, with the majority of this growth concentrated in the new suburbs that were emerging in the fields beyond the old city walls.

To the east of London the small villages along the Thames had been growing steadily since the 16th century and by the 17th century they formed a two-mile-long chain of predominantly working-class "industrial" suburbs. Away from the river the large parish of Stepney with its four hamlets, Ratcliffe, Limehouse, Poplar and Mile End, remained an area of rural farming communities.

To the west there were still significant open spaces when James I came to the throne: apart from buildings along the Strand and around Drury Lane, most of the modern "West End" was undeveloped. The Churches of St. Martin-in-the-Fields (Trafalgar Square) and St. Giles-in-the-Fields (to the south of modern Oxford Street) really were among the fields, and St Martin's Lane was little more than a country track.

Although James I's mother was a Catholic he was brought up a Protestant, and despite the enthusiastic welcome from his new subjects, a group of disaffected Catholics began to plot his assassination. The group was led by Thomas Percy (the cousin of the Earl of Northumberland), Robert Catesby, Thomas Winter and Guy Fawkes. The plan was audacious: the plotters proposed to blow up the King and the Government at the State Opening of Parliament. However the authorities had been forewarned of the plot, and the Parliament building was searched. The gunpowder was discovered, and Fawkes was arrested. He was sent to the Tower of London where he was tortured for three days before finally revealing the names of his co-conspirators, who were executed after a trial at Westminster. Known as the "Gunpowder Plot," the attempt to blow up Parliament is still celebrated in England every November 5th, with fireworks and an effigy of Guy Fawkes which is burned on a fire and the rhyme: "Remember, remember, the Fifth of November! Gunpowder, treason and plot!"

Fines for illicit building

Both James I and his successor Charles I (1625-1649) maintained an official policy designed to curb the city's expansion by requiring people to obtain licenses for any new buildings. But the development of the fields and villages to the west of London into fashionable suburbs was irrepressible. James I believed that the growth of London was so spectacular that in 1615 he claimed: "We found our City and suburbs of London of sticks, and left them of brick, being a material far more durable, safe from fire and beautiful and magnificent."

Elsewhere, less controlled development was going on as people built houses without permission. In 1632 the Privy Council complained about "newly erected tenements in Westminster, the Strand, Covent Garden, Holborn, St. Giles, Wapping, Ratcliffe, Limehouse and Southwark among other places," which they claimed attracted beggars, increased the risk of plague, polluted the Thames and inflated the price of food.

Six years later in 1638 the City authorities could list 1,361 suburban houses that had been built without permission. Both James I and Charles I saw the levying of fines for such illicit building as a valuable source of income and accordingly took payment rather than insisting that these houses be pulled down. In other respects too both James and Charles encouraged development: both kings saw themselves as great patrons of the arts and of architecture, and with their royal architect Inigo Jones (1573-1652) they embarked on ambitious building schemes of their own.

Parliament defies Charles I

James I had to come to the throne on a wave of popular support. However, financial problems and his belief in the Divine Right of Kings (the belief that the king was appointed directly by God and had holy

Inigo Jones was born in London in 1573, the son of a London clothworker. By 1603 he had visited Italy and become an accomplished artist and designer receiving the patronage of Christian IV of Denmark. Queen Anne, the wife of James I and sister of Christian IV, employed him as a designer for court masques. Jones held the post of Surveyor of Works (i.e. architect) to James from 1615 until 1643, building 21 royal buildings, of which only a few remain: the Queen's House at Greenwich (now part of the National Maritime Museum), and the Banqueting House in Whitehall. Between 1634 and 1642 Jones added a magnificent portico on the west front of St. Paul's. With the outbreak of the Civil War Jones lost his position, but although a Royalist he was allowed to live in peaceful retirement until his death in 1652.

PIAZZA in Conventgarden.

In the 1630s the Earl of Leicester acquired land to the West of the Charing Cross Road which would culminate in the 1670s with the laying out of Leicester Square. During the reign of Charles I, the land around Lincoln's Inn Fields was built on and the Earl of Bedford developed Covent Garden market and estate, intended to be "fit for the habitation of Gentlemen and Men of Ability." The architect was Inigo Jones, who was greatly influenced by the piazzas of France and Italy. He produced London's first formal square with stuccoed, arcaded and pilastered houses to the east and northern sides. The garden wall of the Earl's new mansion occupied the southern side and to the west was the church of St. Paul. This was the first Anglican Church to be built in England after the Reformation. The Duke of Bedford did not want to be put to any great expense in the construction of the church. He told the architect that "I would have it not much better than a barn," to which Jones replied, "You shall have the handsomest barn in England!"

authority) slowly began to undermine his popularity.

In 1625 he died, and was succeeded by his son, Charles I (1625-1649). Charles was a quiet and refined man with a stubborn sense of duty. He had a taste for architecture and fine art: he amassed a large collection of paintings and invited both the artists Van Dyck and Rubens to work in England. A deeply religious man, he rejected the austerity of the newly rising Puritan Church, preferring instead the ritual and spectacle of the national High Anglican Church. There was, however, suspicion among many that he wished to restore the Roman Catholic Church in England.

Charles, like his father, had an absolute belief in his divine right to rule. He had also inherited large debts and increasing difficulties with Parliament. Angered by their attitude, the King dissolved Parliament and ruled alone. During this period of "Personal Rule," the king tried to squeeze as much money as possible from London, the largest and richest city in the kingdom. Despite this, Charles never aroused total hostility among London's governing elite. Wisely he never challenged the rights and privileges of the City—instead, in a Charter of 1638 he confirmed many of them.

Charles loses support

But while the Corporation was not entirely hostile, the same could not be said of the citizenry. Many London merchants saw themselves as the victims of the King's constant money-raising schemes, and there existed in the city many agitators

and religious reformers who doubted the King's support for Protestants. After Charles's attempts in 1637 to impose a new church ceremony and prayer book on the Scots provoked riots and the Scottish army invaded the north of England, he was forced to come to terms with Scots. As part of the settlement they required either the occupation of London by a Scottish army or the recall of the English Parliament. The King agreed to call another Parliament. In London the citizens celebrated the news and the Scots were widely regarded as liberators.

The new Parliament met in November 1640. Known as the Long Parliament, it immediately attacked the methods the King had used to raise finances during

The Puritans—seen above burning books after the Civil War—were fundamentalists who opposed the King and the Church of England. They were often sent to jail, whipped, and even hanged. They finally came into power with Cromwell after the execution of Charles I in 1649, and tried to impose a godly pattern of behaviour on the "unruly poor". Other radical groups included the Quakers, Shakers, Ranters and Muggletonians.

5. ỹ Waterhouse

S. Andre in Holborne

his personal rule. Parliament was given a further boost when, despite the royalist sympathies of the Lord Mayor, elections to the Corporation of London led to the appointment of a predominantly Puritan council which was closely allied to the opposition members of Parliament. Charles responded by appointing one of his supporters to the command of the Tower of London garrison.

By the beginning of 1642 the country was gripped by rumors of Catholic and Royalist plots to overthrow the government. The bishops who were supporters of the king and would normally have sat in the House of Lords had by this time become so afraid of the London mob that they dared not come to Westminster. As a result the bishops argued that the Parliament was invalid.

The City and Parliament unite

The King's relations with Parliament and the City continued to deteriorate until Charles declared that his opponents in Parliament were rebels. The English Civil War had begun. In November the Royalist army marched southwards toward London. Parliament put the City into a state of defense: barricades blocked the main approach roads and the militia, or "Trained Bands," were reinforced by the Parliamentary army—a total of 24,000 soldiers were called out.

During the English Civil War, engineers were brought over from Holland to supervise the construction of London's defenses. Everybody was expected to take a share in the work, which was parcelled out between parishes, trades and livery companies—even women and children joined in. The result was an 18-mile defensive trench around the entire city. In addition London built an 18ft rampart mounting 212 cannon. At strategic points along the circuit were 24 wooden forts, each with its own garrison and able to provide support for its neighbor in the event of an attack. The heart of the city they sought to defend is more or less the same as the panorama below in the 1630s, dominated by Old St. Paul's.

The opposing forces met at Turnham Green, only six miles west of London, but the Royalists withdrew without giving battle. London's vulnerability to attack was obvious and Parliament began the construction of a massive defensive system around the City.

London's defenses were never tested. The Royalists never came so close to London again. As the conflict continued and its economic effects began to be felt, many Londoners lost their enthusiasm for the war. In the new year of 1643, several thousand Londoners petitioned Parliament for peace, and in August a mob of women calling for peace stoned soldiers outside Parliament.

In 1645 Parliament raised a new professional army called the "New Model Army." This new force was well trained and well led, easily outmatching anything the king could put against it. In 1646 Charles surrendered to the Scots who handed him over to the English the following year. But there was a real sense of fear that the king would use London's support and the Trained Bands to introduce absolute monarchy. With this in mind and with the New Model Army approaching, the city's Royalist faction dissolved, and the Parliamentary military commander Oliver Cromwell was able to take possession of London without opposition. Although imprisoned, Charles continued to negotiate with the various factions. After a second civil war, the New Model Army occupied the City and Westminster in December 1648, and Parliament was purged of those who favored compromise with the king. At the same time those who favored peace with the King were excluded from elections to the Corporation of London.

At the beginning of 1649, the King was put on trial in Westminster Hall on charges of treason for "levying war against the Parliament and Kingdom of England." Although many Parliamentarians opposed

The Civil War was not a struggle for succession like the Wars of the Roses but a war fought mainly for political and religious ideals. Catholics, High Churchmen, most of the Lords and the old gentry were for the king, while for Parliament were most of the Puritan reformists and House of Commons, the industrial areas, the navy, ports and above all, London, the wealthiest city in the world. After the overthrow of the monarchy, the Parliamentarian military commander Oliver Cromwell (below) swiftly became head of a military dictatorship and called himself the Protector of a united Commonwealth of England, Scotland, Ireland and the colonies. Pictured left is the great Seal of the Commonwelath, representing his reformed House of Commons.

it, the king was found guilty and sentenced to death. He was executed outside the Banqueting Hall in Whitehall (where the crowds could be more easily controlled) on the afternoon of January 30, 1649. With Charles' death, Parliament abolished both the office of King and the House of Lords, and declared England a Republic.

Life in Cromwell's Republic

Under the Republic (1649-1660) and the Government of Oliver Cromwell (1653-1658) an element of stability returned to London. The Puritans closed the theaters, playhouses and bear pits, and suppressed the festivals celebrated on May Day and Christmas but in other respects life continued as normal. Drinking remained as popular as ever and a new fashion was started in 1652 when the first London coffee house was opened in St. Michael's Alley near the Royal Exchange— chocolate was introduced into London at about the same time. Opera and music flourished and were encouraged by Cromwell, dancing was common and the Spring Garden at Charing Cross (replaced in 1661 by the New Spring Gardens at Vauxhall) and the parks

Charles I was executed in front of the Banqueting House in Whitehall. One eyewitness to the event recorded that "there was such a dismal groan among the thousands of people that were within sight of it, as it were with one consent, as I never heard before and desire I may not hear again." Many considered this political act also made Charles a religious martyr, and the execution created criticism that the liberal order for which Cromwell had fought had become impossible—and he was compelled to rule by force and to ruthlessly quash the anarchy and rebellions that followed throughout the Isles.

remained a favorite meeting place for courting couples. In 1658 Cromwell died; he was succeeded as Lord Protector by his son Richard, who lacked his father's ability and took the position unwillingly. Without Cromwell's strong leadership, the country descended into anarchy. At the end of 1659 things came to a head when seven London apprentices were shot dead by soldiers while they tried to present a petition to Parliament.

In February 1660 General Monck, the commander of the English Army in Scotland, marched to London. There in an alliance with the Corporation of the City he restored the members of Parliament who had been excluded in 1648. Parliament then dissolved itself, only to re-form in May 1660 to agree on the terms for the restoration of the monarchy.

Challenges in store for Charles II

Charles I's eldest son was invited to return and take the throne. On May 29 the new king, Charles II (1660-1685), arrived in London. Public rejoicing and civic pageantry greeted him, there were bonfires in the streets and the king inspected his soldiers on his way into London. The scene was vividly described by the diarist John Evelyn, who wrote: "He came with a triumph of over 20,000 horse and foot brandishing their swords and shouting with inexpressible joy. The ways were strewn with flowers, the bells were ringing, the streets were hung with tapestry, and the fountains were running wine. The mayor, alderman and all the companies, in their chains of gold, liveries and banners, were present; also the lords and nobles; the windows and balconies were all set with ladies, trumpets and music, and myriads of people flocked the streets as far as Rochester, so that they took seven hours to pass through the city."

But the new king's capital was sorely in need of development. The Thames still was spanned by only a single bridge and within the city walls London remained a place of

Under Cromwell's rule there was a suprising amount of religious freedom. Independents and dissenters were tolerated and even Presbyterians and Anglicans were left in peace if they were discreet. Even the laws against Catholics were rarely enforced, and in 1655 Cromwell allowed the Jews (expelled by Edward I in 1290) to return to England and in 1657 they built their first new synagogue in London. Jews first settled in London just behind the present location of the Bevis Marks Synagogue—Great Britain's oldest synagogue, in Aldgate (in regular use for weekdays and Shabbat services since 1701)—where they established a kosher butcher, a mikvah, a cemetery, and a small synagogue.

medieval houses, made of timber, around narrow lanes. These were usually cobbled and in a poor state of repair with an open drain running down them that was part gutter, part sewer. The City was, in the words of one historian, an "insanitary, noisome, inconvenient, and overcrowded slum."

London also suffered regularly from that curse of the Middle Ages: the plague. Since the devastating Black Death of 1347-8 London had been frequently troubled by bubonic plague. There had been epidemics in London in 1499 and 1500 and more between 1511-18 as well as outbreaks in various years in the 1530s and 1540s. During a serious epidemic in 1563 the number of burials in London rose eightfold to 20,372 (London's population at the time was probably about 85,000). Between 1563 and 1636 there were a further six outbreaks (roughly one every ten years). While plague never entirely disappeared, after 1636 there were no further epidemics until the Great Plague of 1665, which would be London's last.

The Great Fire

The Plague had declined significantly by September 1666 when one of the greatest catastrophes to hit London would change the city forever. Sometime between one and two in the morning, on Sunday September 2, a fire broke out in the bakery of Thomas Farrynor in Pudding Lane near London Bridge. The baker, his family and servant were forced

The "Grievous Visitation" of the Black Death in 1665 caused Londoners to flee from the city. Carried by fleas living on rats, the plague could come in three different forms: septicemic, where the bacteria entered the blood stream directly and was always fatal usually within hours; pneumonic, spread through sneezing and coughing, this was fatal in about 99 percent of the cases, death occurring within 48 hours; and bubonic, caused by the bite of an infected rat flea. This form caused black swellings or "buboes" in the groin and armpit—it was fatal in about 70 percent of cases with death about a week after infection. The bacterial cause of the disease was not understood, and it was blamed instead on "foul air."

to climb across the roof to a neighboring house to escape the flames. Farrynor's maid was not so lucky and died in the fire.

Like most of the houses in London at this time, Farrynor's bakery and the houses around it were built mostly of timber. The fire spread quickly to the City's busy wharves—"the lodge of all combustibles, oil, hemp, flax, pitch, tar, cordage, hops, wines, brandies and other materials favorable to fire, all heavy goods being warehoused there near the waterside and all the wharfs for coal, timber, wood etc. being in line."

Initially the fire had not been regarded seriously. The Lord Mayor, Sir Thomas Bludworth, had stated that in his opinion a "woman could piss it out." Despite this, within six hours of it starting some 300 buildings as well as the north end of London Bridge were on fire. The authorities now appreciated the danger of the situation and the king gave permission for buildings to be demolished to create a firebreak. But those whose houses were not directly threatened by the fire were unwilling to have their homes demolished, and the fire was spreading rapidly. When Samuel Pepys brought the king's permission to the Lord Mayor, Sir Thomas Bludworth, he describes how the mayor was "like a man spent, with a handkerchief round his neck, to

By the Sunday night of the Great Fire, the diarist and head of customs Samuel Pepys (left), who was watching from a tavern in Bankside south of the Thames, described the scene as "one entire arch of fire from this to the other side of the bridge [London Bridge], and in Bow up the hill, for an arch above a mile long." The fire moved "with such a dazzling light and burning heat and roaring noise by the fall of so many houses together that was very amazing." St. Paul's Cathedral had burned for two days and nights. An estimated 13,200 houses were destroyed.

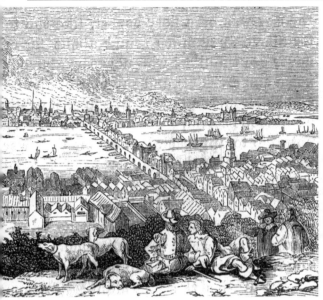

King Charles personally helped to fight the fire together with his brother the Duke of York, who had taken over responsibility for the firefighting. On Tuesday September 4 the fire reached the Guildhall, gutting the building, although London's ancient records in the crypt survived. By the evening the fire had reached St. Paul's Cathedral. Eyewitness John Evelyn wrote: "The stones of St. Paul's flew like grenades, the melting lead running down the streets in a stream, and the very pavements glowing with fiery redness." Fanned by the wind the fire continued westward crossing the River Fleet, where inmates in the Fleet Prison had to be released, and toward the Inner Temple, which also caught fire. On Wednesday the spread of the fire was at last brought under control, the wind that had been fanning and spreading the flames dropped and the clearance of buildings with gunpowder to form firebreaks had some success. During the next two days the fire was at last extinguished although Samuel Pepys wrote that some of the ruins were still smoking in February 1667.

the king's message he cried like a fainting woman 'What am I to do? I am spent! People will not obey me. I have been pulling down houses. But the fire overtakes us faster than we can do it!' "

The fire raged for more than three days and devastated London. Of the 448 acres within London's City walls 373 had been destroyed as well as 63 acres of the suburbs directly beyond the City wall to the west. Medieval London had gone forever. Despite the damage, the fire had destroyed property rather than lives; only nine people are recorded to have died in the fire, but the loss in property was estimated at £10,000,000 (the annual income of the City at this time was £12,000) and John Evelyn estimated that there were "200,000 people of all ranks and degrees dispersed, and lying along with their heaps of what they could save from the fire, deploring their loss."

Some of these people left London forever, others found what shelter they could among the rubble while the rebuilding of the City took place. Immediately following the fire a relief fund was established and donations were received from throughout the country. Although it was vital that rebuilding begin as soon as possible, the authorities

were determined that the rebuilding be properly regulated. The King issued a proclamation promising to build a "much more beautiful City than that consumed" but warned that "the inconvenience of hasty and unskilful buildings must be avoided, and lest should obstinately erect such buildings on pretence that the ground is there own, the Lord Mayor and others are authorized to pull down the same."

Designs for the rebuilding

Within weeks of the fire several grandiose designs for the rebuilding were submitted. These included schemes by John Evelyn and Christopher Wren whose plans involved laying out a new city plan with wide boulevards and piazzas. The schemes were rejected as impractical and too costly. Instead in October a group of Commissioners for Rebuilding were appointed. In February 1667 their suggestions were enshrined as the basis of the Rebuilding Act.

The task of rebuilding the city took over ten years during which time the costs of materials was strictly

Houses were grouped into four categories within which the total height, the number of stories and the thickness of the walls were all standardized. Houses "of the first sort" were built on by-lanes, they could have a cellar, two stories and an attic level; those "of the second sort" which fronted onto "streets and lanes of note" could have three stories in addition to a cellar and attic; those houses fronting onto "high and principal streets" could have four stories, cellar and attic. The London authorities produced a list of which streets belonged in which category, there were six "high and principal streets," 214 "streets and lanes of note" and the remainder were by-lanes. The fourth sort of house dealt with by the act were "mansion houses of the greatest bigness" built for "citizens and other persons of extraordinary quality" but even these, while given more freedom in design had to conform to the building regulations. Overhanging jetties or projecting windows were banned, houses had to be fitted with drainpipes, and buildings had to be constructed in brick or stone.

controlled. The restoration of the Guildhall, the construction of a new Royal Exchange and New Customs House were all accomplished by about 1671. Of the 8,000 houses that replaced those lost in the fire, half were built by 1669 and the rest by 1672.

A Fire Court settled disputes over property boundaries and ownership arising out of the fire. The Court was designed to provide fair and quick judgment and its decisions were final. The responsibility to rebuild was left to property owners and tenants, and the court often would be required to judge financial disputes between them. In 1667 Parliament granted a ten-year tax of a shilling a ton on all coal imported into London to raise money to compensate those who had lost land and to rebuild the city's lost public buildings and prisons. In 1670 a second Rebuilding Act raised the coal tax to three shillings and extended it for another ten years. Half the revenue raised was spent on the rebuilding of the City's churches and St. Paul's Cathedral, the remainder passing to the City to be spent on rebuilding and compensation.

Christopher Wren directs the reconstruction

The task of rebuilding the City's churches and St. Paul's Cathedral was entrusted to Christopher Wren (1632-1723), one of the greatest English architects and a man who more than any other individual is associated with the reconstruction of London after the Great Fire.

In 1669 he was appointed Surveyor of the Works by Charles II. The following year he began the rebuilding of those City churches destroyed by the fire and the building of new St. Paul's cathedral. In 1673 Wren was knighted. During his lifetime Wren was a prolific architect; in addition to his churches his other works included the Customs House of 1669 to 1674 (burned down 1718), Drury Lane Theatre built 1672-74, the Royal Observatory in Greenwich Park built 1675-76, the Royal Chelsea Hospital of 1681-86, and

The Rebuilding Act had also called for "a pillar of brass or stone be erected on or as near onto the place where the said fire so unhappily began as conveniently may be, in perpetual memory thereof." The Monument is sited 202 feet west of the starting point of the fire and takes the form of a single, 202 feet-high column of Portland stone—the tallest isolated stone column in the world.

the Royal Naval College, Greenwich of 1696-1702. By the end of his life Wren is known to have designed 70 buildings in London and has another ten attributed to him. Of these about 50 survive. Wren died in 1723, aged 90, and became the first person to be buried in the new St. Paul's cathedral.

"The Devils take all"

Charles II's relationship with the City had not been an easy one. In his first Parliament in 1661 Charles took control of London's militia, restored the Bishops to the House of Lords, and repealed the Act requiring him to call Parliament every three years. In London it was said, "the Bishops get all, the Courtiers spend all, the Citizens pay for all, the King neglects all and the Devils take all."

In 1668 there were riots when sailors and apprentices attacked brothels in the eastern suburbs, and there was talk among them of pulling down "the great

The foundation stone for the new cathedral of St. Paul's was laid on June 21 1675. Wren (pictured above) was reluctantly forced to demolish Jones' west front, which had been damaged beyond repair in the fire. His new cathedral had a dome capped by a stone lantern supporting a golden cross exactly 365 feet above the pavement. The dome is the third largest in the world, after St. Peter's in Rome and Our Lady of Peace in Yamoussoukro, Ivory Coast.

bawdy house at Whitehall." There was also widespread suspicion that Charles wanted to return England to Roman Catholicism. Although Charles never made a public conversion (instead he converted on his deathbed in 1685) he issued a Declaration of Indulgence, using his own authority (not Parliament) to suspend existing penal laws against Catholics and Nonconformists.

Londoners were increasingly agitated by anti-Catholic sentiment: they published broadsheets and newspapers that circulated in coffee houses and private clubs calling for the exclusion of the king's brother from the succession. It became common for an effigy of the Pope to replace Guy Fawkes on the fires lit for the Gunpowder Plot celebrations. In November 1679, Lord Shaftesbury the leader of the Whig Party organized a massive celebration on the anniversary of the accession of Queen Elizabeth I when effigies of the Pope were traditionally burnt and two weeks later the London mob turned out to welcome the Duke Monmouth, who as the illegitimate son of Charles II was an alternative Protestant claimant to the throne.

Between 1670 and 1680 an opposition party (who enjoyed the support of the City of London) known as Whigs, gradually developed in Parliament. Those who supported the government of Charles II became known as Tories. The Tories also enjoyed some support in London and caricatured

the Whigs as republicans and anarchists who wanted to destroy the monarchy and the established church. Both sides used mass meetings, pamphlets and political clubs to put their message across—it was the politics of the crowd, and it is no coincidence that at this time the word "mob" (pictured above apprehending a political victim) entered the English language.

Fear of Catholic power

Unlike Wren, Charles II did not live to see the completion of St. Paul's Cathedral. He died in 1685, and was succeeded by his brother, the Duke of York, who became James II (1685-1688). James outwardly favored Catholics in positions of state and government. In 1685 following disputes with Parliament, he began his own period of personal rule. In 1687 he ordered that a Declaration of Indulgence for Catholics be read from all church pulpits; when seven bishops refused they were imprisoned in the

Tower of London. When the bishops were subsequently acquitted there were celebrations in London.

Within three years James had alienated many of his subjects who as Anglicans disliked and feared his Catholic policies. Nevertheless many were willing to tolerate the king as the next in line was James' Protestant daughter by his first wife, Mary.

However in June 1688 James' second wife, the Catholic Mary of Modena gave birth to a son, which meant that James would

be able to leave a Roman Catholic dynasty on the throne. Although James attempted to win the favor of London by restoring the City's Charter, the birth of a Catholic heir was simply too much for the majority of Anglicans. Negotiations were opened with James's daughter Mary and her husband William of Orange in July 1688.

Religious uncertainty over the monarch's allegiance continued when seven bishops defied James II's order to read the Declaration of Indulgence—ordering the people to tolerate Roman Catholics. They were at once taken to imprisonment in the Tower.
Below: The staunchly Protestant William and Mary.

The Glorious Revolution

In an event known as the Glorious Revolution, William and Mary were invited to invade and in November William landed with his army in Devon. So many of his Protestant officers had deserted to William and Mary that James was unable to offer any resistance and fled to France. On the way he dropped the Great Seal of State into the river Thames. It was found five months later by a fisherman.

William entered London at the beginning of

Ciuitatis Weftmonafterienfis pars.

Parlment Houfe   The Hall   The Alby

Sala Regalis cum Curia Weft-monafterij   anglice Weftminster haull

December 1688. Parliament was called in January 1689 and in the following month it declared that by his flight James II had abdicated and offered the vacant throne to William and Mary.

The offer of the throne came with conditions: only Parliament could pass laws, raise taxes, and decide foreign policy, members of parliament (MPs) all had to be members of the Church of England, the monarch had to be a Protestant, and there was to be no standing army in peace time. Both William and Mary accepted these conditions, which established Parliamentary sovereignty and the constitutional monarchy in England. They were crowned William III (1689-1702) and Mary II (1689-1695) respectively on April 21 1689.

Two views of the Houses of Parliament and Westminster in 1647. Crucially, the great Fire of London had only struck the City and so Westminster and its buildings escaped damage. "The Hall" or Westminster Hall still survives. Built in 1097, it housed the Law Courts until 1882, and it was here that many famous figures were condemned to death, such as Thomas More, Anne Boleyn, Guy Fawkes, and King Charles I.

Reigning not ruling

In the relative peace and prosperity that followed the Glorious Revolution and the establishment of Parliamentary supremacy in England and Scotland, William and Mary were the first English monarchs who could be said to reign but not to rule. London underwent a Commercial Revolution. The city had for many years driven the economies in its surrounding area, but by the end of the 18th century the London market was becoming all-embracing, seeking trade from every corner of the nation and overseas.

POLITICAL RAVISHMENT ... or ... The Old Lady of Threadneedle Street in danger!

By 1650 it has been estimated that the London trade in Newcastle coal directly employed 8,000 people. By the end of the 17th century one contemporary remarked that "there is no county or place in England but directly supplies London, or at one hand or other supplies them that do supply it." As the trade through London increased, a system of credit based on bonds or bills of exchange evolved, which in turn developed into an elementary banking system and ultimately led to the formation of the Bank of England.

Although Charles II continued to borrow from the Corporation of London, the new bankers were becoming increasingly important to the royal finances. In 1672 when Charles (who by then was over a million pounds in debt to 14 London bankers) was refused any further loans to fund a war against the Dutch, he ordered the Exchequer to stop

Medieval monarchs had looked to the local Jewish community or Italian merchants for extra finance. The Tudors had turned to the money markets of Antwerp when the Crown needed to borrow cash, but James I and Charles I consistently raised funds through loans from London, granting tax monopolies or giving land in return. Ultimately however, the poor record of the Crown in repaying its debts led the City of London to refuse loans to Charles I. As the country drifted toward the Civil War, Charles seized the mint at the Tower and gained control of the country's stock of gold. As a result some of London's goldsmiths took on the role of financiers paying interest on bullion deposited with them, which they then lent on to Parliament. The goldsmiths would run accounts for their depositors and would issue their own bills, effectively acting as bankers. These goldsmith-bankers continued to operate after the Restoration, often specializing in the lending and borrowing of money, which had originally been just a sideline, such as Child's, Hoare's, and Snow's.

repaying the his existing debts and used the money instead to fund the war.

Rise of the stock market

At the same time as these developments were taking place in banking, a trade in stocks and shares was beginning to develop in London. Dealing in stocks

By 1677 there were about 40 goldsmith-bankers operating in London. In 1694 the Government agreed to establish a national bank. A consortium of City merchants and financiers undertook to

and shares took place in the Royal Exchange or one of the nearby coffee houses, John Houghton described the London trade in stocks in 1694: "The monied man goes among the brokers which are chiefly upon the exchange or at Jonathans Coffee house sometimes at Garraway's and at some other coffee houses and asks how stocks go and upon information bids the broker buy or sell so many shares of such and such stock."

In 1696 a Parliamentary enquiry into "the pernicious art of stock jobbing" led to the expulsion of the brokers from the Royal Exchange. Instead, they set up shop at Jonathan's Coffee House, which thus became the direct ancestor of the London Stock Exchange. In the same year, Parliament introduced an act to regulate the trade, claiming that brokers had "carried on most unjust practices and designs in selling and discounting of talleys, bank stock, bank bills, shares and interests in joint stocks and other matters and things, and had unlawfully combined and confederated themselves together to raise or fall from

loan the government £1,200,000 in return for interest of 8% paid from "rates and duties upon the tunnage of ships and vessels and upon beer and ales and other liquors." The new "Bank of England" (England's first joint-stock bank) operated from the Hall of the London Company of Mercers, before eventually getting its own building in Threadneedle Street where it remains today. It is sometimes referred to as "the Old Lady of Threadneedle Street"— pictured in the satirical cartoon opposite.

Overleaf: Frost Fair on the frozen Thames in winter 1683.

Along with the rise of the banks and the stock market, commercial insurance rapidly saw its development to a form we would recognize today. During the 1680s the coffee house of Edward Lloyd became a popular haunt for ship owners, sea captains and merchants. At Lloyd's the merchants and ship-owners could all be found in one place. Lloyd, who took no part in the insurance deals that were conducted in his coffee house, provided a congenial atmosphere and premises for merchants and ship owners to meet and discuss business. He also provided reliable shipping news, he first issued his *Lloyds News* in 1696, which was the forerunner of *Lloyds List*. In the comfort of the coffee house the merchants did business each taking a share of the risk, they would sign their names to a policy one under the other and for this reason were known as underwriters. Lloyd died in 1713, but his name remained associated with London's marine insurance market. By 1720 Lloyds had moved to the Royal Exchange along with the London Assurance and the Royal Exchange Assurance.

time to time the value of such talleys, bank stock and bank bills most convenient for their own private interest and advantage." But attempts to control them failed and there was a massive rise in the number of brokers. By 1714, the terms "bull" and "bear" in reference to brokers were already in common usage.

Debts and orphans

Ironically as London developed as a safe place for the nation's money market, the Corporation of London was plunged into financial crisis. It had been customary that when a Freeman of the City died, if he had children under 21, a third of his personal estate would be held by the city in trust for them until they came of age; this was called the Orphans Fund. This money was held by the city in a single fund along with the City's other income. From this same fund the City made all its disbursements.

By the second half of the 17th century the City's income had dropped dramatically as a result of the civil war and restoration, the plague, the Great Fire, and the various court actions fought over the suspension of the City Charter. As the City's debt began to rise, the number of children requiring payment from the Orphans Fund increased; by 1684 the amount required was £500,000. The City could only afford to pay the interest on the outstanding amount. In 1694 with the debt at £700,000 the City was forced to go to Parliament for help. Parliament issued the Orphans Act, all the City's debts were consolidated and an additional duty was placed on coal and wine entering the City to pay off the balance. The City would not recover from her debts until the middle of the 18th century; her financial prestige, however, would never be quite the same again.

Despite the upheavals of the 17th century, this was a time when culture and science thrived. Between 1648 and 1659 a group of academics had held regular scientific meetings at the University in Oxford. With the restoration the group based itself in Gresham College London, which had been founded in 1579 by Thomas Gresham to give free lectures in the subjects of Divinity, Music, Astronomy, Geometry, Physics, Law and

The Royal Exchange Assurance also offered fire insurance. The concept of fire insurance was established immediately after the Great Fire when Nicholas Barbon, a builder and speculator, established the "Fire Office," offering insurance against fires—with distinct rates for brick and timber dwellings, and often with a clause that he should undertake the rebuilding of fire-damaged properties. Other companies followed, some setting up their own fire services. Insured properties were identified by metal badges fixed to the walls and the various fire brigades would only fight those fires in properties insured by their own company. Some of these companies also offered life insurance. Pictured left is Newgate Prison set ablaze in 1780 as mobs claimed the streets during the Gordon Riots. Above is "The Golden Boy of Pye Corner," a golden statue that commemorates the "staying of the Great Fire" and symbolizing gluttony, seen as one of the fire's causes.

Rhetoric. In 1660 the group which included
Christopher Wren and Robert Hooke (who
discovered the law of elasticity) and Robert Boyle, the
chemist, formed a society, and were given a Royal
Charter in 1662 becoming the Royal Society Of
London For The Promotion Of Natural Knowledge,
but known simply as the Royal Society. Other
members included Isaac Newton who was elected in
1671 and Edmund Halley the astronomer, in 1678.
The Royal Observatory also was established under

The Royal Observatory
at Greenwich was
commissioned by Charles
II in 1675 and designed
by Wren. Its original
purpose was to apply the
new knowledge of
astronomy to problems
of maritime navigation.
The first Astronomer
Royal was John Flamstead
who organized the staff

and prepared very
accurate star maps using
the instruments shown
here. Flamstead's
successor was Edmond
Halley (above, top), a
contemporary of Isaac
Newton (above). The line
of longitude running
thorough the observatory
is still used as the "prime
meridian" from which the
rest of world sets its time.

Charles II with the appointment of John Flamstead (who was also a member of the Royal Society) as Astronomer Royal. The Observatory was housed in a purpose-built building designed by Christopher Wren in Greenwich. But Royal generosity did not extend to the astronomer's instruments and Flamstead had to buy his own!

Rising from the ashes

The years between the accession of James I and the death of William III in 1702, at the very beginning of the 18th century, were tumultuous. The political conflict and revolutions in the reign of Charles I and James II ensured parliamentary supremacy in England (and later the United Kingdom).

Physically London had changed. The suburbs had mushroomed, though there still was much greater expansion to come over the next two centuries, James I had boasted that he had rebuilt London in brick and stone. Following the Great Fire of 1666, which swept away the old medieval city, London really was rebuilt. Inigo Jones and Christopher Wren, the two architects who oversaw the transformation of London, would set the architectural fashion in England for years to come.

During this period firm foundations were laid for the massive cultural, economic and population changes that would take place in London in the centuries to follow.

Though always courting controversy, the later years of Charles II's 25-year reign proved to be something of a Golden Age for London. The early years, however, had proved inauspicious: an appalling plague hit the country in 1665 with 70,000 dying in London alone, and the Great Fire of London in 1666. Meanwhile, a war with the Dutch led to New Amsterdam in the new territories of America being renamed New York and culminated in a Dutch attack on the Thames in 1667. Peace was negotiated later that same year.

CHAPTER 7

THAT GREAT SEA
THE LONG 18TH CENTURY 1688-1837

"In London, that great sea, whose ebb and flow, At once is deaf and loud, and on the shore, Vomits its wrecks, and still howls on for more. Yet in its depth what treasures!"

—Percy Bysshe Shelley

Letter to Maria Gisborne
(1820)

George I (right) was brought over over from Hanover, Germany, to become king of England at the age of 54. Rather than a hindrance, the German's deliberate ignorance of the English language and customs actually became the cornerstone of his style of rule from 1714-27: leave England to its own devices and live in Hanover as much as possible — as evidenced by this satirical scene (left) of Beert Street that shows how confident Londoners took the greatest relish in blurring the distinction between work and pleasure.

Q UEEN MARY II DIED IN 1695 and William III ruled alone till his own death in 1702. The throne then passed to James II's daughter, Anne (1702-1714). Whitehall Palace had been destroyed by fire in 1698, and never had been rebuilt. Instead William III had redeveloped Nottingham House into Kensington Palace for his own use. Anne however chose to establish her court at St. James's Palace (where she had been born in 1665). After the death of her husband in 1708, she took up permanent residence at the Palace and began a program of modernization and restoration. St. James's would remain the principal London home of the monarchy throughout the 18th century and into the 19th, when the Royal Family took up residence at Buckingham Palace.

During her brief reign Queen Anne had little personal impact on London, but her Parliament passed the two London Building Acts of 1707 and 1709. These revolutionized the architectural styles of buildings in London and effectively established the "Queen Anne" style in domestic architecture in both England and the colonies. The style would dominate

London in

River Thames

The Act of Union in 1707 in the reign of Queen Anne united England and Scotland to form the country of Great Britain (Ireland joined the Union in 1801 to create the United Kingdom). This had little immediate impact on the capital. Pictured left is a view of the bustling St. James's Palace during Anne's reign.

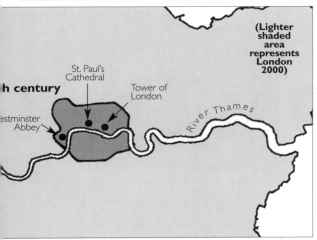

St. Paul's Cathedral

Tower of London

(Lighter shaded area represents London 2000)

h century

estminster Abbey

River Thames

English domestic architecture until the 1720s when it gave way to the Georgian town house.

Parliament also passed the 50 Churches Act of 1711 that allowed one final flourish of the Baroque style in London. The aim of the act was "the building of 50 new churches in or near the Cities of London or Westminster or the suburbs thereof." The act further specified "churches of stone and other proper materials with Towers or Steeples to each of them." The churches were to be paid for by a tax on coal. The act was a response to the need for new churches as a result of the growth of the suburbs as well as fear over the increase in the number of dissenting chapels being founded in the East End. In the event only 12 churches were ever built.

The Act of 1711 was the first time since the Great Fire that architects had been given the opportunity to build in London on such a scale. Two surveyors (or architects) were appointed to design the new churches. Nicholas Hawksmoor designed half of the churches built, while the other post was ultimately held by several notable architects including Thomas Archer and James Gibbs.

London in the Long 18th Century not only expanded rapidly but also saw a new style of architecture that was to set the standard for the following centuries. Since the Great Fire, the 1667 Rebuilding Act had regulated buildings in the city. This had laid down specifications that had enshrined the best practices of the period, dictating that houses had to be of brick, with a specific thickness of wall and number of floors, but it made no mention of exterior design and decoration. Like the 1667 Act, the Acts of 1707 and 1709 were aimed at reducing the risks of fire. In 1707, the wooden eaves-cornices fashionable on buildings of the Restoration period were outlawed. In response builders introduced a cornice of stone, brick or stucco and placed a low parapet around the roof to afford it some protection. The 1709 Act specified that windows were no longer to be flush with the outside wall of the building but had to be set back into the window embrasure by four inches. This was made possible by the adoption of the sliding sash window—a lasting feature of British architecture since that time.

Gibbs published two books—*A Book of Architecture* (1728) and *Rules for Drawing the Several Parts of Architecture* (1732)—which, along with his church St. Martin's-in-the-Fields, became profoundly influential. The design of St. Martin's inspired the design of churches throughout the British empire but especially in New England and Canada. By the 1720s the Baroque style was going out of fashion, in favor of a far stricter adherence to classical forms in architecture as expressed by the works of the Italian Renaissance architect Andrea Palladio (hence Palladianism). The Palladian movement rejected the baroque of Wren and his successors, and instead looked back fondly to the works of Inigo Jones. Palladianism would be the dominant architectural fashion for much of the 18th century, before it gave way toward the end of the century to Neo-Classicism, a form that drew directly from ancient classical architecture rather than later Renaissance interpretations of it.

"Whither will this monstrous city?"

The early years of the 18th century saw another period of rapid growth for London. By the 1720s when Daniel Defoe described London, in his book *A Tour Through the Whole Island of Great Britain*, the City had long since spilled beyond her city walls.

The London that Defoe found was a large

Nicholas Hawksmoor (1661-1736; left) was a student and collaborator of Wren's, and he had also worked closely with the imaginative and original Baroque architect Sir John Vanburgh (1664-1726). The first church Hawksmoor designed for the 1711 scheme was the Church of St. Alfege in Greenwich, built between 1712 and 1718, followed by several more. In his designs, Hawksmoor rejected traditional thinking, and instead he experimented with space, distorting squares along various axes to give shape to his churches. On the exteriors he blended a mix of Classical and Gothic motifs. Inside, the churches are purposefully light, spacious and airy. But his most familiar work is the twin towers he added to the west front of Westminster Abbey in 1735-45.

metropolis (it was still only about four miles from east to west, compared with 18 miles in 1900). He wrote "that Westminster is in a fair way to shake hands with Chelsea, as St. Giles is with Marylebone; and Great Russell Street by Montague House, with Tottenham Court: all this is very evident, and yet all these put together, are still to be called London. Whither will this monstrous city then extend?" Defoe thought that the development of London was so dramatic that there were "new squares, and new streets rising up every day to such a prodigy of buildings that nothing in the world does, or ever did, equal it." This development was the result of speculative building.

It was claimed that during the 18th century a man needed only £100 to set up as a speculative builder. In reality the potential returns were so great that many small craftsmen were tempted to enter the business with insufficient capital. One commentator, writing in 1747 about bricklayers who set themselves up as master-builders in the speculative trade, recorded that: "It is no new thing in London for these Master Builders to build themselves out of their own Houses and fix themselves in jail with their own materials."

These men were not professional builders nor financiers, but wealthy or well connected individuals who could afford to speculate in the hope of high financial rewards. However none could compare to

For the 1711 Act, Thomas Archer (1668-1743) designed St. Paul's, Deptford (1712-30, below left)—perhaps the most beautiful of the Baroque churches—and St. John's, Smith Square, Westminster (1714-28). Another influential architect, James Gibbs (1682-1754), built St. Mary-le-Strand (1714-17). But it is for the rebuilding between 1722 and 1724 of St. Martin-in-the-Fields, Westminster (below), that Gibbs is best known. It cost £33,000—not as part of the 1711 Act but at the request of the parishioners whose church was no longer "in-the-fields" but at the heart of a busy and elegant new suburb.

the financier and builder Nicholas Barbon, the father of fire insurance, who as speculative builder mass-produced houses often to a standard pattern. Barbon was a ruthless developer. When he acquired the Tudor palace of Essex House on the Strand he discovered that the king wanted to buy it back. In order to prevent the king from forcing him to sell, he dug up the garden and pulled down the house before the king could act. In another incident, when he developed Red Lion Square near Gray's Inn, he led his laborers in a pitched battle against the Inn's lawyers who had come out to forcibly stop the development.

The years between 1689 and 1713 saw a slowdown in the growth of the suburbs. This was a period of almost continual warfare, with England involved in the War of the Grand Alliance (1689-97) and then the War of the Spanish Succession (1702-13) against France. Both these wars led to conflict in American continent where they are known as King William's War and Queen Anne's War.

Avalanche from east to west

When peace arrived, London started expanding once

more. In the 17th century those people with sufficient wealth to move out of the eastern parts of the City and suburbs started to migrate to the new, smarter suburbs in the west. In 1694 the German J. W. Archenholtz wrote: "Within the space of 20 years, truly a

Thomas Wroithley, the fourth Earl of Southampton, established a trend when he developed Bloomsbury in the early years of the Restoration. He granted leases on the land with the condition that the lessee would build a house or houses on the land at his own expense; however, these would become the property of the ground landlord (in this case the earl) when the lease ran out. This system had the benefit of allowing hereditary landowners to develop their property with the minimum of expense and without selling it or dividing it. Those who purchased the leases were also speculators, effectively middlemen who had no intention of living in the houses that they built, but who constructed them for others to rent or buy. By the 18th century the system was becoming more refined. Where Southampton had granted leases of 42 years, by the turn of the century leases of between 60 and 64 years were more common, and by the end of the century 99 years was usual. It became normal to encourage developers by charging ground rent on a sliding scale, with the initial charge being very low.

migration from the East End of London to the west, thousands passing from that part of the city, where new buildings are carried on, and to this end, where fertile fields and the most agreeable gardens are daily metamorphosed into houses and streets." Thus by the 18th century this movement was rapidly becoming an avalanche. By the end of the century, the eastern suburbs had taken on a distinctly working-class character, and were increasingly home to waves of immigrants.

In the poorer suburbs where income was low and leases were short, the quality of the speculative development was predictably poor. It was not uncommon for new houses in these areas to collapse before they were even occupied. Older tenements and houses were often subdivided to accommodate several families; in 1801 a physician at the Public Dispensary claimed that "from three to eight individuals of different ages often sleep in the same bed; there being in general but one room and one bed for each family. The room occupied is either a damp cellar, almost inaccessible to light, or a garret with a low roof and small windows."

With peace, development began again, concentrated along the Tyburn Road (now Oxford Street). The area to the south was attractive as it was close to both Westminster and St. James's Palace, and it was here that the first great developments of the 18th century occurred: George Street and Hanover Square (pictured above and named in honor of George I [1714-1727] and the new Hanoverian dynasty), Savile Row, Brook Street, New Bond Street, and Berkeley Square, which rapidly became one of the most desirable addresses in London.

Overleaf: Detail of the City of London and Westminster in the 1740s.

The most ambitious development was the 100-acre estate laid out between 1720 and 1780 and centered on Grosvenor Square. By the time building finished, 1,375 houses had been built, as well as two chapels and a workhouse. Today only two of the original buildings survive. One of these, No. 9, was the home of John Adams (1735-1826), where the second President of the United States lived while ambassador to the Court of St. James. But the US connection did not end there: in 1938, the United States Embassy was established on the east side of the square. After the Second World War, the U.S. Government asked the Grosvenor Trustees to sell them the freehold to the western side of the square for a new embassy building. The trustees agreed, on condition that 12,000 acres of Grosvenor land in Florida confiscated during the War of Independence be restored. Understandably the U.S. Government refused, and it is said that this is the only American embassy where the U.S. does not own the freehold.

It was also common for such rooms to be rented on a nightly basis. In 1753 the High Constable of Holborn, commenting on the lodging houses in his district, wrote: "There have within a few years arisen in the outskirts of this town a kind of traffic in old ruinous houses which the occupiers fill up with straw and flock beds, which they nightly let out for twopence for a single person or three pence for a couple."

There were some speculative schemes of quality housing in the East End such as Wellclose Square by the London Docks, which was laid out at the end of the 17th century and intended for prosperous sea captains. Between 1768-74, the well-known architect Charles Dance the Younger laid out a grand housing scheme to the north of the Tower of London comprising The Crescent, The Circus, and America Square (probably so named because it was home to merchants and sea captains involved with trade to the American colonies). Elsewhere too in the east there were pockets of wealthy merchants and prosperous artisans, but the majority of development was of the poorer sort.

Gulf between the suburbs

As the East and West End suburbs developed the gulf between them became increasingly obvious, writing in 1794, Archenholtz wrote: "The East End, especially along the narrow shores of the Thames, consists of old houses, the streets are narrow, dark and ill-paved; inhabited by sailors and other workmen who are employed in the construction of ships and by a great part of the Jews. The contrast between this and the West End is astonishing; the houses here are mostly new and elegant; the squares are superb, the streets straight and open .·. . if all London were as well built there would be nothing in the world to compare with it."

The growth of the suburbs south of the Thames was much slower. Tanneries had become established in Bermondsey, and there were timber yards as well as Delft and stoneware potteries in Lambeth. Much of the land south of the river was marshy, or given over to market gardens and agriculture. The growth of the southern suburbs was boosted from the middle 18th century by the construction of two new bridges over the Thames; Westminster and Blackfriars. Other bridges followed: Vauxhall Bridge (also called the Regent's Bridge), which was London's first iron bridge built 1811-16; Waterloo Bridge (originally called Strand Bridge) 1811-17; and Southwark Bridge between 1815 and 1819. At Hammersmith a suspension bridge was built to help speculative development south of the Thames between 1825-27. The medieval London Bridge was cleared of its remaining buildings and given a new central span between 1758-62. A new bridge finally replaced it in 1824-31.

At Spitalfields there was substantial growth. Writing in the 1720s, Daniel Defoe described the East London area as "all those numberless ranges of building called Spittle Fields, and well inhabited with an infinite number of people." After 1685 Spitalfields became home to the Huguenots, Protestant refugees fleeing religious persecution in France. In Spitalfields they established a silk-weaving community, building distinctive terraces of houses (below). The area remained poor and non-conformist. Spitalfields had the first Baptist Church to be built in England in 1612. In 1684 it was observed that the area was the "most factious hamlet of all the Tower Division, having had many conventicles in it."

Migrants lured by prosperity

By the time the 1801 Census was taken, the south London suburbs were home to one-sixth of the population of London. Between 1650 and 1801 the number of Londoners grew from 400,000 to 959,310; despite this dramatic rise the population constantly remained at 11 percent of the total English population. By 1811 the population stood at 1,139,355 and in 1831, six years before the Victorian Age, the population had reached 1,655,582. When the growth of London's population is matched against the city's birth and death rates it becomes clear that the rise in population had to be caused by people coming into the city.

It has been estimated that London was receiving a constant supply of about 9,000 people a year to maintain her 18th-century population rise. Most of these migrants came from the counties and towns around London and were often young, unmarried

By the beginning of the 18th century the need for a bridge across the river at Westminster was obvious and despite vigorous opposition from the City and the Thames Watermen who operated the existing ferries, Parliament passed the Bridge Act in 1736 and a lottery was held to raise funds. The bridge was opened in 1750. Further down-river, at Blackfriars, the Corporation built a toll bridge between 1760 and 1769, pictured during its construction, showing the temporary footbridge. Originally called William Pitt Bridge, to the public it was always Blackfriars Bridge. It was freed from tolls in 1785.

men and women drawn to London in the hope of finding good jobs and high wages. Of the people treated at the Westminster Dispensary between 1774 and 1781 only a quarter were London born, 58 percent English or Welsh migrants, 8 percent were Irish, 6 percent were Scots, and 2 percent were from elsewhere. The Irish population in London in 1780 probably numbered about 20,000.

Migrants from beyond the kingdom included the French Huguenots, 13,500 were known to have arrived but the actual number could be double that. Many settled in Spitalfields and Soho (there were 14 Huguenot churches in Soho).

The Jews also formed another major group of immigrants. Oliver Cromwell had allowed the Jews to return to England during the 17th century; these had been Sephardic Jews from Spain and Portugal. In the early 18th century there was an influx of Italian Jews including one Benjamin D'Israeli whose grandson,

Entrance to a synagogue by a pub in Leadenhall Street, during the 18th century when the Jewish community was starting to make a significant impact on the growing fortunes of the City.

also named Benjamin, would become prime minister. While the first two waves of Jewish immigrants had usually found work as craftsmen and artisans or among the growing number of London's financiers and bankers, the next group were by contrast desperately poor. These were the Ashkenazi Jews who arrived from Eastern Europe from the middle of the 18th century. By 1700 there were probably about 8,000 Jews in London; a hundred years later one contemporary estimated that there were between 15,000 and 20,000 Jews in the city.

At this time London was also home to a small African-Caribbean/American population. By the 1650s London was heavily involved in the transatlantic slave trade. It was not uncommon for merchants, naval officers and colonial officials to return to England bringing their slaves with them. If the slaves ran away and were recaptured they would be returned to their owner. However, in 1772, the case of a runaway Virginian slave called James Somersett was brought before the Court of Kings Bench. The Judge, Lord Justice Mansfield, ruled that the "pure air" of England and slavery were not compatible and that "as soon as a slave sets his foot on the soil of the British Isles he becomes free."

In 1787 the Society for the Abolition of the Slave Trade was formed. In 1807 the slave trade was declared illegal within the United Kingdom, and by 1838 slavery was abolished throughout the British Empire. The size of London's black population is not known; it certainly increased in the 1780s with the arrival of African-American soldiers who had fought on the British side during the American War of Independence. During the Mansfield case it was argued that there were about 15,000 slaves in Britain and that the total population, including freemen, was about 20,000, of whom about half lived in London.

London prospered from the slave trade, and many slaves ended up there rather than the New World. Olaudah Equiano (Gustavus Vassa) wrote down this experience. Kidnapped from West Africa at the age of eleven, he was shipped to the West Indies and sold to a Virginia planter. After ten years of enslavement throughout the North American continent, Equiano bought his freedom. At the age of 44, he wrote and published his autobiography in London, The Interesting Narrative of the Life of Olaudah Equiano, Or Gustavus Vassa, The African. Written by Himself (1789). More than two centuries later, this work is recognized not only as one of the first works written in English by a former slave, but, perhaps more importantly, as the paradigm of the slave narrative, a new literary genre.

Golden Age of Georgian architecture

Despite the large number of speculative development schemes in London in the early Hanoverian period there was not a great deal of public-funded building during the reigns of either George I (1714-1727) or George II (1727-1760). However from the late 1750s onward the number of public building built in London increased dramatically, and this period has been called the Golden Age of Georgian architecture. Robert Adam and his brother James became the pioneers of Neo-Classical style of architecture, which eventually displaced Palladianism.

The most ambitious building scheme of the period did not come from the Government, nor from private landowners but was the result of Royal speculation and had George, the Prince of Wales and his architect John Nash (1752-1835) as the developers. Prince George had become Regent in 1811 during the madness of his father, George III. This grand scheme included the building of Regent's Circus (now Piccadilly Circus), from which a wide curved road with a graceful colonnade (Regent Street) ran north to the junction of Oxford Street, where Nash built his second circus, Oxford Circus. The road then runs north again, cutting through Port-land Place before reaching Park Crescent and Park Square. At this northern end of the scheme Nash landscaped Marylebone Park to create Regent's Park named in

The Adam brothers were kept busy in the West End, building the spectacular Adelphi Terrace (1768-74) on the Strand near Charing Cross, and Portland Place (1776-80). Between 1776-86, William Chambers rebuilt Somerset House (below) as government offices in a Classical Palladian style. Other public building works of this period include the Bank of England 1767-70 (rebuilt 1788-1833), while the Royal Mint on Little Tower Hill was built in 1807-9. Before this, England's coins had all been minted in the Tower of London. The present-day Canadian Embassy, or Canada House, in Trafalgar Square was built originally for the Royal College of Surgeons (1824-27).

honor of its patron, the Prince Regent. The park was flanked to the south, east and west by a group of stucco rendered terraces designed by Nash and looking like palatial mansions. To the north the park was ringed by the Regent's Canal (constructed 1811-1820) and the scheme incorporated a canal basin and a working-class district and market to the east. Nash's new road

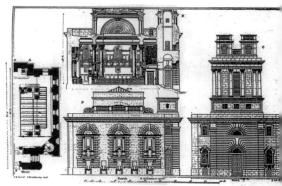

sliced the West End into two, and divided the poorer working district of Soho from the wealthier aristocratic district of Mayfair. It has continued to be a divide between rich and poor to this day.

In 1830 George IV died, and Nash retired with some of his schemes unrealized. Nevertheless his work in the West End remains one of the most successful pieces of urban planning in modern London's history.

But some found the rapid development of London and its suburbs alarming and feared the future. At the outbreak of the American War of Independence in 1776, the writer Horace Walpole believed that everything, even London itself, was about to collapse, writing: "As its present progress is chiefly north, and Southwark marches south, the metropolis promises to be as broad as long. Rows of houses shoot out every way like a polypus; and so great is the rage of building everywhere, that, if I stay here a fortnight, without going to town, I look about to see if no new house is built since I went last. America and France must tell how long this exuberance of opulence is to last! The East Indies, I believe, will not contribute to it much longer. Babylon and Memphis and Rome, probably, stared at their own downfall. This little island will be ridiculously proud some ages hence of its former brave days, and swear its capital was once

There was a renewed wave of church-building in London with the 1818 "Million Church" Act, providing one million pounds to build churches throughout the country. The Act was in part an expression of thanks for England's victory over France at Waterloo and the end of the Napoleonic wars. The Government was also worried about religious dissent, so the new churches, which were all Anglican, were built "lest a godless people might also be a revolutionary people." Each church had to accommodate "the greatest number of persons at the smallest expense." That meant one church for about 2,000 people at a cost of no more than £20,000.

as big again as Paris—or what is to be the name of the city that will then give laws to Europe—perhaps New York or Philadelphia."

Docks grow along the Thames

One great stimulant to the growth of London's East End suburbs was the development of London's docks. A law of 1558 had established 17 legal wharves along the north bank of the Thames in an area between London Bridge and Limehouse Reach, an area known as the Pool of London. In the 17th century the number of wharves was increased to 20 and a series of "sufferance" wharves were established, mainly on the south side of the Thames.

By the beginning of the 18th century Daniel Defoe "found above 2,000 sail of all sorts, not reckoning barges, lighters or pleasure boats, and yachts" waiting to be unloaded in the Thames. By the 1750s London was handling a vast tonnage of imports; the trade with the East Indies required 8,000 tons of shipping per year, with the American Colonies, who sent over tar, pitch, tobacco,

rice and timber, 88,000 tons of shipping was required. A further 47,000 tons of shipping was needed to import sugar from the West Indies and the timber trade with Norway and the Baltic required 263,000 tons of shipping. But imports from overseas were dwarfed by London's consumption of coal, which was brought from the north of England by coastal vessels. In 1700 London imported about 400,000 tons of coal a day; by 1800 this had grown to just under one million.

In 1820, when the Prince of Wales became King George IV (1820-1830), he and Nash planned more luxury developments in central London. Nash set to work rebuilding the royal residence at Buckingham House, turning it into Buckingham Palace (pictured in 1852). In front was a massive monumental gateway; as Marble Arch, this was removed to Hyde Park in 1847. Nash extended Pall Mall to Charing Cross, and at the junction of Pall Mall, Whitehall and the Strand, he built a magnificent new square, called Trafalgar Square in honor of Admiral Horatio Nelson's great naval victory of 1805. Nash's square was empty: Nelson's Column was added to the Square in 1839-42, the Lions in 1867, and the fountains in 1939.

By the late 18th century, congestion on the river was appalling with ships moored in the Thames forming a line stretching for two miles above London Bridge and for four miles below it. It was not unknown for ships to remain caught in the congestion for weeks. Those ships that were too large to enter the Pool of London were still forbidden to unload and had to discharge their cargo into smaller vessels for unloading at the official wharves. Nevertheless, in spite of all these difficulties, London's trade was expanding rapidly and the city was becoming phenomenally rich. In 1700 the value of London's import and export trade stood at about £10,000,000. By the mid-1790s this had grown to about £31,000,000.

Cheesemongers and cabinetmakers

The Thames provided jobs for many Londoners but away from the river there was a wealth of trades and occupations operating in the city. Different areas of London increasingly were becoming associated with particular trades or occupation. Spitalfields was associated with the manufacture of silks and there were cheesemongers and cabinetmakers in St. James's and the cabinetmaker Thomas Chippendale had a workshop in St. Martin's Lane. There were clockmakers and poulterers in Hanover Square, and Clerkenwell was becoming famous for precision instruments, jewelery and watches, as was Shoreditch. There were watermen and laborers in the streets around Westminster Abbey, Covent Garden had its carriage makers and was notorious for prostitutes. The building and fitting out of ships took place along banks of the Thames to the east of London and the dockyards of Woolwich and

In response to the accelerating growth in trade in the Port of London, in 1798 Dr. Patrick Colquhoun, a magistrate and author of *A Treatise on the Police of the Metropolis*, formed the Marine Police Force, the first organized police force in Britain. A year later, the West India Company managed to dig its own dock on the Isle of Dogs—the West India Docks—in 1802. It was possible to unload a ship in just four days. Alongside the docks were bonded ware-houses for storage, and a massive wall to prevent theft enclosed the whole complex. In 1805 the London Docks at Wapping were given a 21-year monopoly on all imports of rice, tobacco, wine and brandy from Europe and North America. Other docks built included the East India Docks, St. Katherine's Dock, and the Surrey Commercial Docks. A network of canals also sprang up to service the new docks.

Deptford both employed about 900 people. South of the Thames, Lambeth was becoming associated with the manufacture of pottery and the lumber trade and Southwark and Bermondsey with leather and tanning.

City of shopkeepers

Where there are lots of manufacturers there also tend to be lots of retailers. By the end of the 18th century London was also a city of shops. These were highly decorated with large amounts spent on their fittings. Defoe wrote in 1713: "It is a modern custom to have tradesmen lay out two-thirds of their fortune in fitting up their shops. By fitting them up, I do not mean furnishing their shops with wares and goods to sell; but in painting and gilding, fine shelves, shutters, boxes, glass doors, sashes, and the like, in which they tell us now, 'tis a small matter to lay out two or three hundred pounds."

The shops themselves were quite small but where possible they would have had large bay windows to show off their goods. Each shop would have a wooden sign board or hanging symbol to represent their goods, but these were eventually banned in 1762, as a danger to the public if they collapsed. In 1784 Sophie de la Roche, a German visitor to

In the list of voters in Westminster in 1749, 395 different occupations were listed, including 846 victuallers, 491 tailors, 379 carpenters, 300 peruke makers (wig maker), 285 shoemakers, 271 butchers, 269 chandlers, 183 bakers, 141 distillers, 88 chairmen (people who carried sedan chairs), 83 laborers and 41 watermen. In 1791 the London Directory for the City listed 14,744 merchants, tradesmen and master craftsmen, about 1,000 civil servants, 1,840 attorneys, 81 rectors or vicars, 479 surgeons and 86 apothecaries. It is believed that there were as many as 32,000 women, mostly unmarried girls under the age of 25, working as servants in London between 1695 and 1725, compared to about 8,000 male servants.
Overleaf: An 18th century view of London Bridge shortly before the demolition of the houses lined along it.

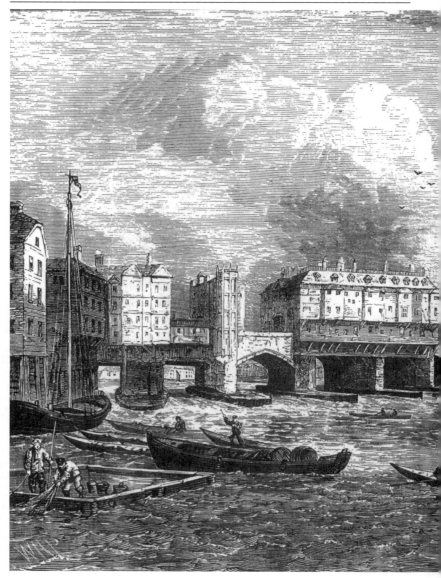

London, wrote: "Behind the great glass windows absolutely everything one can think of is neatly, attractively displayed, in such abundance of choice as to make one greedy." And the Frenchman Pierre Grosley considered that London's shops "make a most splendid show, greatly superior to anything of the kind in Paris." It was not just in shops that 18th century Londoners could spend their money. By the end of the 17th century the coffee house had joined the tavern as a popular venue for relaxation. There were about 3,000 coffee houses in London during the 18th century.

But by the beginning of the 19th century the coffee house as an institution was in decline. The reason was probably little more than a change in fashion. Those with wealth and opportunity could easily join one of the many private clubs that were being formed at this time. Workers, tradesmen and artisans could just as easily congregate in the many taverns.

Soccer and boxing

John Strype writing in 1720 described most popular pastimes for Londoners as "football [soccer], wrestling, cudgels, ninepins, shovelboard, cricket, stowball, ringing of bells, quoits, pitching the bar, bull and bear baitings, throwing at cocks and lying at alehouses." And a commentator writing 20 years later added "sailing, rowing, swimming and fishing in the

A contemporary observer wrote: "These coffee houses are the constant rendezvous for men of business, as well as the idle people so that a man is sooner asked about his coffee house than his lodgings." The coffee house was like a business club or venue for the gathering of like-minded people. Aside from Edward Lloyd's coffee house, there were others such as Will's, a resort of men of letters and was the haunt of the poets Alexander Pope and John Dryden. One commentator described the coffee houses in the West End in 1714: "You are entertained at picquet or basset [card games] at White's [pictured left], or you may talk politics at the St. James's. The political parties have their different places, where however a stranger is always well received; but a Whig will no more go to the Cocoa-tree [a choco-late house] than a Tory will be seen at the coffee house St. James's. The Scots go generally to the British, and a mixture of all sorts to the Smyrna. Young Man's for officers, and Little Man's for sharpers [rogues and card cheats]." Many coffee houses served as receiving houses for the Penny Post, which would deliver letters.

Thames, horse and foot races, leaping, archery, bowling in alleys, and skittles, tennis, chess, and draughts; and in the winter skating, sliding and shooting" to the list. Boxing too was popular and by 1780 a boxing school had been established in Whitechapel.

Another entertainment was a visit to see the inmates of the Royal Bethlehem Hospital, better known as Bedlam. The hospital was open to the paying public who would tease and bait the inmates. By 1770 admission was by ticket only but in 1815 the practice was abandoned. Fighting and baiting with animals would attract large crowds, but by 1800 these entertainments had become increasingly working-class. In 1833 cock fighting was banned, and bull and bear baiting were similarly dealt with shortly after. Horse racing became popular toward the end of the century and the Oaks and Derby were first run in 1779 and 1780. But nothing drew a larger crowd in London or gave a more enjoyable outing than a public execution.

Spectacle of public executions

Up to 1783 public executions took place at Tyburn (near Hyde Park on the site of the Marble Arch) where the triangular "triple tree" gallows could hang eight people from each beam. On the day of an

Away from the taverns and coffee houses Londoners could enjoy the pleasures of one of London's three royal parks: St. James's Park, Green Park, and Hyde Park. Often crowded on Sundays when Londoners would take the air, of the parks St. James's was the oldest. Formerly a royal hunting ground, Charles II had it landscaped, but it became the haunt of prostitutes and street gangs, even though it was illegal to draw a sword in the park. By the 1750s, the Park had been restored although it remained a haunt of prostitutes. Green Park, opened by Charles II, was never quite so popular. Hyde Park, like St. James's, was once a hunting ground. It became the most fashionable of the parks, and was also popular with highwaymen. In a bid to deter them, William III had 300 gaslights installed, but with little success. Next to Hyde Park was Kensington Gardens, the grounds of Kensington Palace, which George II opened to "respectably dressed people." To the north, Regent's Park was built as part of John Nash's Metropolitan Improvements in the 1820s. Pictured is Hyde Park Corner in 1750 with the park behind it.

execution the condemned individuals were trans-ported, usually three to a cart, which they shared with their coffins, the three miles from Newgate Jail. The route was always crowded and there was even a stand called Mother Proctor's Mews where the paying public could get a better view. If the condemned was a famous or notorious criminal, young woman or a highwayman, crowds of over 30,000 people might gather, and the largest recorded was about 80,000.

The sight of the crowd could sometimes lead to bravado from the condemned who would often wear their best clothes, or were encouraged to make dramatic gallows speeches. It was not unknown for the crowd to riot when a last-minute pardon stopped the entertainment. *The Foreigner's Guide to London* of 1740 described the scene "the rope being put about his neck, he is fastened to the fatal tree when a proper time being allowed for prayer and singing a hymn, the cart is withdrawn and the penitent criminal is turned with a cap over his eyes and left hanging about half an hour." After their execution the bodies were sent for dissection and it was not uncommon for

The number of capital crimes increased from 50 at the beginning of the 18th century to about 200 by the turn of the 19th. On average only 35 criminals were hanged each year in London and Middlesex, although there were two occasions in the 1780s when the totals almost reached 100. The illustration above shows a condemned man being taken to be hanged at Tyburn. Hanging was the principal form of execution from Anglo-Saxon times up to abolition of the death penalty in 1964. The greatest number of hangings took place at the gallows of Tyburn, near what is now Marble Arch, at the end of Oxford Street.

a criminal's friends and family to fight the soldiers guarding the execution for possession of the corpse. It was partially as an attempt to control the crowd that executions were moved to Newgate Jail in 1783. Public executions continued till 1868 when an Act of Parliament finally banned them.

The "Thief-takers"

The number of executions may well have been higher had London had a more advanced system of policing. In 1700 law and order in the capital was still maintained by a system that had been set up in 1285. Initially this was for the defense of the City, but by the 16th century with less need for defense it took on a policing role. The Watch Act created a de facto paid police force in 1737. In 1748 the novelist Henry Fielding was appointed a magistrate at Bow Street. He established a force of six volunteer "thief-takers"; they wore no uniforms and were unpaid but allowed to keep any reward money. Initially called "Fielding's People," by the turn of the century they were known as the "Bow Street Runners." In 1805 the Bow Street Horse Patrol of 60 men was established against an increase of highway robberies (the last mounted highway robbery was recorded in 1831).

Despite the recruiting of more Bow Street Runners by 1818 it was becoming obvious that the system needed reforming.

The last beheading on Tower Hill took place in the 18th century; this was the execution of Lord Lovat in 1747. Stands had been erected around the scaffold to allow a better view, but one collapsed, killing twelve people. It was said Lovat smiled at satisfaction at the spectacle. He was not however the last person in England to be executed by beheading —in 1820 five of the "Cato Street" conspirators, who had planned to assassinate the Cabinet, were beheaded at Newgate, not with an ax but with a surgeon's knife. Lesser criminals were frequently put into the stocks or pillories (below), but this was dangerous because of the fruit and vegetables thrown by the public.

The Home Secretary, who now had responsibility for the policing of London, had a total of no more than 400 officers for a city now numbering over one million. In 1828 the Home Secretary, Robert Peel, introduced a London Police Bill into Parliament, though following opposition from the Corporation the square mile of the City was excluded. The Bill passed into law the following year as the Metropolitan Police Act. Although the Bow Street Runners and the Thames Police retained their independence for another ten years, the Act established a new force of 3,000 men under the command of two Commissioners.

The headquarters for the new London force was Scotland Yard, in Whitehall. In 1842 a new Detective Department was formed with two inspectors and six sergeants. Each policeman—now called a "Peeler"—was issued a blue uniform and top hat; the uniform was especially designed not to look military. In 1839 the City finally followed suit, and the City of London Police were established for the Square Mile. Even today the Metropolitan Police and the City Police remain two separate forces.

Henry Fielding's Bow Street Runners were at first nicknamed "Robin Redbreasts" on account of their scarlet waist-coats, the original six Bow Street Runners were London's first band of constables. Below is the interior of Bow Street police office in about 1816. They were not confined to London and traveled all over the country in search of criminals, gaining a reputation for honesty and efficiency. Fielding used his writing skills to produce a bulletin called *The Weekly Pursuit*, which circulated throughout England and gave details of stolen goods and suspects. Later renamed *The Hue and Cry*, it is still published under the title of the *Police Gazette*.

The "right" to riot

One obstacle to those who wished to establish a police force in London was the belief held by most Londoners that they enjoyed ancient liberties and a long tradition of freedom and that any police force could be used to deprive Londoners of their "liberties" and to establish French-style absolutism. During the 18th century London was not a revolutionary city in the same way as Paris, Philadelphia and Boston, although the Government constantly feared that the London Mob could erupt into revolution.

Instead, Londoners tended to strike and riot. It often took little provocation to provoke a riot among people with little other way of expressing themselves. At this period the franchise only extended to those people who met a specific property or wealth qualification. The majority of those living in the City and its suburbs had no right to vote. The exception to this was wealthy Westminster where voters were actually in the majority.

Riots could be a form of protest, like the Gin Riots of 1737 sparked by the government's attempts to regulate and tax the sale of gin (Londoners drank 8 million gallons of gin a year before 1751 when another Gin Act reduced consumption to 2 million gallons a year). Politics was another popular cause for disturbance; elections were often followed by riotous behaviour, and there were frequent outbreaks of street battles between mobs of Whigs and Tories.

Another favorite was the theater riot. It was so common for audiences to express their opinions through rioting that both the Covent Garden and Drury Lane theaters had iron spikes fitted along the

Above: Members of the theater-going public storm the stage half-way through an opera (Arne's *Artaxerxes*) in Covent Garden, 1763. The reason this time was because of public disgruntlement over changes in the price of admission, but the theater was a place where any disagreement in the audience could spill over onto the stage. Theater managers had their work cut out in dealing with the rowdy elements who turned up and demanded to be entertained.

Overleaf: Londoners make merry in Cheapside on Lord Mayor's Day, 1761.

stage to guard against hostile audiences. Bad performances and unpopular actors, especially French actors, or a change in seat price could all spark a theater riot. So common were these disturbances that following a riot in 1738 at the Haymarket Theatre, when the audience objected to the presence of French actors, the judge told the court that "the public has a legal right to manifest their dislike to any play or actor." In 1755 a disturbance at Drury Lane occasioned by the presence of French ballet dancers led to a pitched battle among the audience, who ripped out the benches and destroyed the scenery, causing £4,000 worth of damage. The tradition of rioting continues today, such as the Poll Tax Riots of 1990 and the Stop the City riots in 1999.

Protest over work conditions

The most common causes of unrest were disputes over employment, pay or conditions. Between 1717 and 1800 there were 120 strikes in London. Workers often attacked factories, equipment and warehouses, as well as strikebreakers. On other occasions they would riot against cheap immigrant workers, usually from Ireland, brought in by employers to break strikes and force down wages.

Disturbances could focus on religion, such as those that followed the suspension of the chaplain of St. Saviour's Church in Southwark, following an inflammatory sermon. Fires were lit in the streets and several Dissenters Meeting Houses were attacked. Far more serious was the anti-Catholic Gordon Riot of 1780. Led by the young Scots nobleman and MP, Lord George Gordon, a crowd of about 6,000 people marched on Westminster to protest against Parliament's lifting of restrictions on Catholics. As evening fell troops were called to disperse the crowd and the mob began a campaign of destruction of Catholic property. For five days the riots continued, however after a few days the rioters began to attack symbols of the establishment. 210 rioters were shot dead, a further 75 died in hospital and 173 others were treated for wounds. 450 people were arrested of whom 160 were brought to trial, 25 were hanged and 12 were imprisoned. Despite the damage, estimated at over £100,000 not a single Catholic was killed.

There were further smaller riots in 1720 and again in 1739 when troops were once required to restore the peace. A mob smashed engine looms in 1763 and two years later about 8,000 weavers marched on Westminster. In 1769 the weavers again rioted, attacking looms and killing one person in a shooting incident. Once again the Government sent in soldiers to restore order, and two of the leaders of the riots were hanged. That same year in the riverside districts of Shadwell and Wapping, gangs of striking coal-heavers attacked taverns, and once again order was not restored until the authorities stationed guards along the riverfront.

Voice of the Radicals

Against this background of riotous behavior there was a growing mood of radicalism among London's enfranchized small merchants, master craftsmen and artisans. Unlike the 17th century when the City had been involved in opposition politics the radical opposition

It was the silk weavers of the East End who most frequently resorted to riot as a form of expression. Framework knitters rioted in 1710 over a dispute about the number of apprentices being taken into the industry. Nine years later the Spitalfield silk weavers rioted in protest over the growing fashion for printed calico. They attacked women seen wearing calico in the streets, and it was not uncommon for them to have their clothes ripped from them. After two of their leaders were arrested some of the rioters attempted to march on Lewisham where a calico printing press had been established. Meanwhile in the City the Lord Mayor ordered that the city gates be closed and the trained bands to be assembled. A troop of Horse Guards was detached to patrol Spitalfields and soldiers were sent to head off the rioters. The soldiers were able to disperse the rioters but not before one of the weavers was shot dead.

of London during the 18th century was driven largely by the voters of Westminster and Middlesex. Londoners found political champions in the persons of William Beckford and John Wilkes. William Beckford (1709-1770), an Alderman and twice Lord Mayor, was elected to Parliament in 1754, where he allied himself with William Pitt (1708-1778), prime minister from 1757-1761. Pitt resigned from office in 1761 and in the election that followed Beckford stood as a radical in opposition to the new administration. He called for shorter Parliaments, a wider franchise, and an end to "pocket boroughs," those boroughs which returned Members of Parliament but were under the control, "in the pocket," of a single family or person, or, as he described them, "little pitiful boroughs send members to Parliament equal to the great cities."

When in 1775 rebellion finally broke out in America the colonists enjoyed considerable support in London, and the city presented two remonstrances to the government in favor of the Americans asking that the government consider the damage that any conflict with the colonies would create in Britain and referring to the ancient liberties of Englishmen.

The City even received a letter from the Committee of Association of New York asking that London use all its efforts to restore honor and peace. The City responded by issuing another remonstrance calling for an end to hostilities. Shortly after the Committee of Philadelphia appealed to the City as the "Patron of Liberty" to negotiate with the king for peace. But neither the king nor the government would consider a settlement with the colonists. The City, worried both by the damage to trade and the

John Wilkes (1725-1797) was elected to Parliament in 1757, where he quickly became an associated with a loose group of radicals who opposed the government known as the "Patriots." This name would later be adopted in the American Colonies by opponents to George III, who saw links between themselves and the radicals in Britain. After a controversial but colorful political career, which saw him repeatedly elected to parliament while declared an outlaw or imprisoned by the State—most notably for calling the king a "liar"—some of his influential supporters, including several MPs, formed in February 1769 the Society of Supporters of the Bill of Rights. Initially the Society aimed just to pay off Wilkes's debts, but it soon became a radical society organizing meetings and publishing pamphlets. In 1773 the Society had drawn up an eleven-point list of aims, which included minor reforms of Parliament as well as a call for the restoration of fiscal rights to the frustrated American Colonies.

The 18th century saw an explosion of highly influential writers such as Jonathan Swift (pictured below). Their activities led to the founding of a newspaper industry based in Fleet Street (left), such as *The Morning Post* in 1772, and *The Times* in 1788. Pictured above is an edition of the first daily newspaper, *The Daily Courant*.

destruction of liberty in what they regarded as a civil war with the American Colonies issued a public address. They wrote: "We lament the blood that has been already shed; we deplore the fate of those brave men who are devoted to hazard their lives—not against the enemies of the British name, but against the friends of the prosperity and glory of Great Britain; we feel for the honor of the British arms, sullied—not by the misbehavior of those who bore them, but by the misconduct of the Ministers who employed them, for the oppression of their fellow subjects; we are alarmed at the immediate, insupportable expense and the probable consequences of a war which, we are convinced, originates in violence and injustice, and must end in ruin." At the same time petitions calling for peace were sent to both the House of Lords and House of

Commons. In March 1776 the Common Council again approached the King calling for reconciliation and peace; the King's reply was that he would show clemency "as soon as the rebellion was at an end." Three months later the Declaration of Independence was signed.

London still hoped for reconciliation so when in early 1778 the government called for public subscriptions in support of the war the City of London refused to give anything. In the summer of that year, however, France declared its support for the colonists and declared war on Britain; Spain followed the following year. With the widening of the conflict support for the colonists in London became difficult to justify and opinion rallied behind the government.

On the brink of change

Despite the occasional civil disorder between the death of William III and the accession of Victoria, the period was one of great wealth and development in London. By the middle of the 1830s London stood on the brink of change. The Industrial Revolution had not really affected the city, as the great breakthrough and developments had occurred

As the city's population increased there was a rise in the educational needs of the population. University College in 1826—"for the youth of our middling rich people"—and King's College in 1828, were built (both now part of the University of London). There was also a growth in paternalism expressed through the formation of "The Charitable Society for Relieving the Sick, Poor and Needy" in 1716 and the foundation of new hospitals, including St. Thomas' Hospital, rebuilt 1693-1709, Guys Hospital in 1725 (pictured above), St. Bartholomew's, rebuilt 1730-31, the London Hospital founded in 1740, and the Middlesex Hospital in 1745.

elsewhere. But the effects of the revolution were soon to be felt in the capital.

Two events can be seen as symbolizing this change; in 1834 the ancient Palace of Westminster was destroyed by fire. To rebuild it, Parliament chose the architect Charles Barry (1795-1860). Barry was instructed that the new building was not to be based on the classical styles of Greece and Rome, which had been the fashion for 200 years, but in the new Gothic style. Here indeed was a break from the past.

Then in 1836 the London & Greenwich Railway Company opened the first passenger railway in London, between Deptford and Spa Road, Bermondsey. Ten months later the company opened their temporary terminus at London Bridge.

This first railway line was hardly impressive despite being built on a splendid brick viaduct for its whole length of about four miles. But it was the beginning; the railways would eventually change London out of all recognition. On June 20 1837, King William IV died at Windsor. His 18-year-old niece Victoria succeeded him. A new age—the Victorian Age —had dawned.

The period was also a time of flourishing in the arts and education: the British Museum (left) dates from 1753 when the physician and antiquary Sir Hans Sloane left the nation his collection in return for £20,000. To this was added 6,000 manuscripts collected by Robert Harley, Earl of Oxford, and a set of manuscripts from Sir Robert Cotton, and 9,000 books from the Royal Library presented by King George II. This vast array was established as the British Museum in Bloomsbury and opened to the public in 1759. The Dulwich Picture Gallery was opened in 1813, the National Gallery was founded in 1824, and even the Tower of London got a new museum in 1825. **Overleaf:** The river front of Hammersmith, from the eyot at Chiswick to the bridge, 1800.

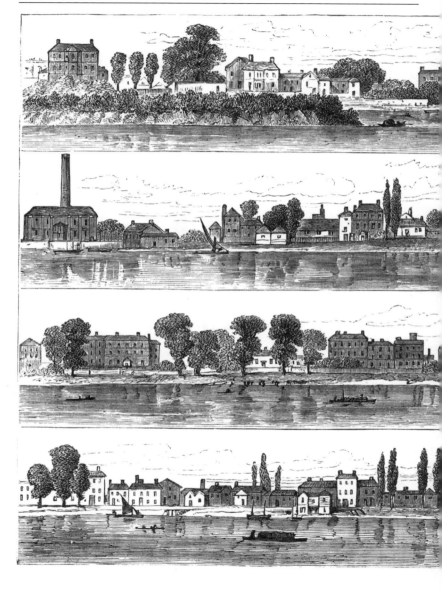

CHAPTER 8

METROPOLIS OF EMPIRE

VICTORIAN LONDON 1837-1901

"But what is to be the fate of the Great Wen of all?
The Monster, called 'the Metropolis of the Empire'?"
—William Cobbett, *Rural Rides* (1822)

"And so through all this I came to love this dreadful
ant-heap, where every night a hundred thousand
men know not where they will lay their heads, and
the police often find women and children dead of
hunger beside hotels where one cannot dine for
less than two pounds."
—Alexander Ivanovich Herzen
Memoirs (1852)

In 1801, when the first British census was taken,
the population of London (including the suburbs)
was just under a million people at 959,310. Four
years after Queen Victoria came to the throne,
the 1841 Census showed London to have a
population of 1,949,227. When Victoria died 60
years later in 1901, the population of London was
4,536,267. As for the modern Greater London
area, in 1801 the population was 1,096,874,
increasing a hundred years later to 6,506,889.

DURING THE YEARS 1837-1901 London underwent the most dynamic period of growth in its entire history. But the city did not grow from the center as a uniform and planned entity. Instead speculative housing sprang up randomly and tentacles of ribbon development reached outward to outlying towns and villages. The great building booms of the 18th century had been largely confined to Westminster and the areas immediately adjacent the City. Daniel Defoe had described London as a "monstrous city" and a "vast mass of buildings" yet it would have been possible to walk from east to west across Defoe's London in an afternoon. Just over a hundred years after Defoe wrote those words, Henry Mayhew viewed London from a hot air balloon, and reported: "It was impossible to tell where the Monster City began or ended for the buildings stretched not only to the horizon on either side, but far away into the distance."

Despite London's huge size the city lacked any form of central government. During the 18th and 19th centuries, local administration tended to be exercised at parish level. The City itself was governed by the Corporation of London, the term for the combination of the Lord Mayor, the Court of Common Council and the Court of Aldermen. By the 1830s the word "Metropolis" began to be used in reference to London for the first time, and "Metropolitan London" was increasingly seen as a single entity. Various commissions

The Victorians made the 19th century an incredible period of activity on every level. London itself grew proportionately to the rapid expansion of the British Empire overseas—meaning that just as the Empire was the greatest the world had even known, London became its greatest city. This was not without its cost, however, and the abject poverty and near slavery of workers in the capital were comparable in many ways to their counterparts in the colonies, provoking waves of reforms.

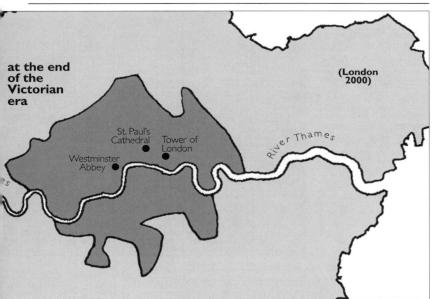

at the end
of the
Victorian
era

(London
2000)

River Thames

St. Paul's
Cathedral

Tower of
London

Westminster
Abbey

were organized to look into the question of providing
a single unitary authority for the city. But little was
done and in the mid-1850s London still was
administered by about 300 different bodies with
about 10,000 members.

In 1855 spurred on by the need to take action to
halt a devastating outbreak of cholera, Parliament
passed the Metropolis Local Management Act. The
Act swept away all the various different parishes,
commissions and boards who had been responsible
for local administration—with the exception of the
City, which retained its independence—and replaced
them with 38 local authorities. In 1886 the newly
elected Conservative Government began to plan the
formation of a system of County Councils
throughout the nation. London was incorporated into
the scheme, and when the Local Government Act was
passed in 1888, the London County Council (L.C.C.)
was formed.

The imagination of Victo-
rian Londoners was captured by public monuments,
such as that to the admiral
Lord Horatio Nelson, raised
on a pillar in the newly
designed Trafalgar Square.

The City was given the status of a "borough within a county," and retained a certain amount of independence but had to contribute financially to L.C.C. costs and projects. The L.C.C. was elected by all of the voters of London and took over in 1889 with responsibility for parks, drainage, transport, roads, paving, bridges,

asylums and entertainment licenses. In 1899, London's government was again reformed with the passing of the London Government Act, which created 28 Metropolitan Boroughs.

Revolution in the transport network

Perhaps the single biggest engine for London's metropolitan growth in the 19th century was the revolution in the city's transport network that, for the first time allowed workers to live beyond walking distance from their employment. At the turn of the 19th century the most common method of traveling around London, other than walking, was by the short-stage coach, Hackney coach or steamboat.

Overheads for the short-stage coaches were high with the result that their fares were generally quite expensive. The journeys were often slow and uncomfortable. One French passenger who took the coach into London from Richmond, in 1810, recorded that "we stopped more than 20 times on the road, the debates about the fare of one-way passengers, the settling themselves, the getting up,

The Victorians made the 19th century an age of technical achievement. Just as in the 20th and 21st centuries, new improved ways of travel were potent symbols. Pictured above is a trial trip by steam locomotive on a shallow stretch of the new Underground railway in 1863. One of the main architects in every sense

of the burgeoning rail system was Isambard Kingdom Brunel (right), an engineer whose influence on the face of London had as much impact as that of Wren.

and the getting down, and the damsels showing their legs in the operation and tearing and muddying their petticoats, complaining and swearing, took an immense time. I never saw anything so ill managed. In about two hours we reached Hyde Park Corner!"

Another widely used form of transport was the Hackney coach. First used in London in the 17th century, it was drawn by two horses, had four wheels and could carry six people. The name Hackney was derived from the French word *haquenée*, meaning a "pacing horse." In 1814, the innovative "chariot" had also become popular. This could take two people inside with a third sitting outside. In 1823 the "cabriolet" was introduced from France. With just two seats and one horse, it charged a lower fare than either the coach or the chariot. This had a folding hood, but was open at the front so passengers often got wet in bad weather. Each of these needed a license to operate, and in the 1820s there were 1,100 licensed coaches and chariots, and 165 cabriolets. As well as roads, the Thames provided a popular highway into London. The first passenger steamboats had begun operating on the Thames as early as 1815.

The Omnibus

In 1829, George Shillibeer, inspired by the sight of the vehicles in Paris, introduced the omnibus to London.

In 1825 there were about 418 short-stage coaches operating in the City, making a total of 1,190 journeys a day. In addition there were about 600 coaches operating from the West End making 1,800 daily journeys. The coaches had between four and six seats inside and could, with four horses, carry 12 people on the roof. Pictured is a steam-carriage from 1828.

The modern London "black cab" is the direct descendant of the Hackney coach (below left, 1842), and each still has to obtain a "Hackney carriage license". Below right is a Hansom cab (also 1842).

By the 1840s the capacity of the omnibus had been significantly increased by the development of the knife-board seat that allowed passengers to be seated in safety on the roof. In 1842, The Times described omnibuses as "lumbering, clumsy conveyances in which the public were packed like coal sacks and jolted through the streets."

Shillibeer's omnibus (after a while this was abbreviated to simply "bus") was little more than a box on four wheels, drawn by three horses. A door at the rear gave access and two benches along each side allowed 20 passengers to be seated. There were soon several omnibus companies operating in London.

But at sixpence a journey, the initial fares were too high to be afforded by the working classes, in 1837 one writer observed that the omnibus was used by "the merchant to his business, the clerk to his bank or counting house, the subordinate official functionaries to the Post Office, Somerset House, the Excise, or the Mint, the Custom House or Whitehall, persons with limited independent means of living, such as legacies or life-rents, or small amounts of property; literary individuals; merchants and traders small and great; all in fact who can endeavor to live some little distance from London." But after a brief price war, the penny fare was introduced attracting the working classes to the omnibus.

Thames river boats were often overloaded, especially in the summer, and accidents were common. The worst took place in September 1878 when the steamer Princess Alice collided with the coal steamer Bywell Castle off Woolwich; there were only 69 survivors from the accident, the death toll was estimated at 640.

In the 1850s there was a growing movement to introduce trams into London. Those who favored the tram—at first horse-drawn —were able to point to the success of the vehicle in North America. As the engineer W. Bridges Adams explained to the Royal Society of Arts in 1857: "Once familiarized with railway carriages drawn by horses, the observant American mind was not slow to perceive that the arrangement was very superior to omnibuses for town transit." In 1861 the appropriately-named American George F. Train established three trial horse-drawn tram routes in central London. His tramways had to be removed after only a few months since the routes he had chosen ran through wealthy suburbs where the inhabitants only used private transport. Although his venture failed, the idea of introducing trams into London would not go away, and in 1869 Parliament agreed to the building of more tram lines in the East End and south of the Thames.

Age of railway mania

The omnibus and the tram were not the greatest agents for change in 19th-century London; instead, it was

the railways that had the greatest impact. In February 1836 the London & Greenwich Railway Company opened London's first passenger railway between Deptford and Bermondsey. Ten months later the line was extended to a new terminus at London Bridge. Lines were soon opened throughout the rest of the

Trade generated by international exhibitions and the abolition of toll roads in 1864 gave public transport a boost, which was helped in the 1870s by a fall in the price of horse fodder and an end to the mileage tax on omnibuses. Despite a growing number of competitors, including the new underground railways, the omnibuses maintained an average of 40 million passengers a year. By 1895 there were 12,236 omnibuses operating in London. By 1875 there were also 348 horse-drawn trams running along carrying 49 million passengers a year. Tram fares were controlled by Parliament, and they had, by law, to operate a "workman's service" between 5 and 7 o'clock in the morning at a penny with a halfpenny charge per mile thereafter. On the return journey, workers could use any tram that ran after 6 o'clock in the evening. Unlike the railways, the introduction of trams did not push the boundaries of the suburbs outwards, although as the suburbs expanded, the tram network increased to service them. There remained large gaps in the network as no trams were allowed in the City or Westminster.

London and connected up with the other parts of the country. North of the Thames, the London & Birmingham Railway opened its terminal at Euston in 1837, and the Great Western Railway opened its terminal at Paddington in 1838.

In 1846 Parliament set up a Royal Commission on Metropolitan Termini to regulate railway building in London. Both the Government and the Corporation of London were of the opinion that in order to minimize traffic congestion in the City railway terminals should all be sited outside the central area. This effectively meant London would never get a major, truly central station. Despite the restrictions

London's first passenger railway, between London and Greenwich (intially from Spa Road to Deptford), was built on a brick viaduct for its whole length, lifting it out of the marshy ground in Deptford. The company opened a pedestrian walkway into London alongside the line that could be used for a penny —120,000 people walked the route in 1839. The railway was

placed on them this was a time of railway mania with new stations and connections continuing to be built every year. As a result of the 1846 decision, Fenchurch Street was now one of the most central termini in London, followed by Waterloo Station in 1848, and King's Cross in 1852.

In the 1860s the authorities finally agreed to stations being built within the previously restricted area of the City, resulting in the opening of Cannon Street (1866) and Liverpool Street (1874). Serving the West End were Victoria Station (1860) and Charing Cross in 1864.

popular from the start: it was direct and 15 minutes quicker than road transport. In its first week it carried 700 people a day, by 1844 it was carrying about 2 million passengers a year. The line was extended in 1838 eastwards to Greenwich where omnibuses from Blackheath, Lewisham and Woolwich would meet every train.

Going underground

The ban on the construction of railway stations within the central London area had been an attempt to control traffic congestion but it was obvious by the 1850s that it had failed. In 1855 a Parliamentary Select Committee on Metropolitan Communications recommended that the main railway terminals should be "connected by railway with one another, with the docks and the post office." The result was a decision to build two underground railways. In 1863-65 the first was opened by the Metropolitan Railway Company connecting Paddington Station to Liverpool Street via the railway stations of Euston and King's Cross.

The new underground railway was an instant success despite the opinion of *The Times* newspaper which had written in 1862 that it was an "insult to common sense to suppose that people who could travel as cheaply to the City on the outside of a Paddington bus would ever prefer, as a merely quicker medium, to be driven amid palpable darkness through the foul subsoil of London."

In fact passengers were pleasantly surprised. One passenger wrote of a journey taken in January 1863 that "we experienced no disagreeable odor, beyond the smell common to tunnels. The carriages hold ten persons, with divided seats, and are lighted by gas; they are also so lofty that a six-footer may stand erect with his hat on." By the end of its first year of operation the railway had carried nearly nine and a half million people and taken over £100,000 in ticket sales. Once again the familiar pattern of rapid expansion followed: similar lines were built across the capital and beyond to create what is still one of the world's most extensive underground systems.

New roads to tackle traffic congestion

Despite the construction of the underground railways, road traffic continued to increase. Although

The new station of Charing Cross in the heart of the West End destroyed the ancient Hungerford Market built in 1662. In front of the station, the railway company built a replica of the medieval Eleanor Cross that had given the area its name. The original cross was one of a series of crosses built by Edward I in 1290 to mark the stopping places of the cortege that brought the body of his beloved wife, Queen Eleanor, from Nottinghamshire to Westminster Abbey for burial. Edward built 12 crosses (of which only three now survive). The South Eastern Railway's cross is actually a romantic replica based on old prints.

there was some new road construction in the mid-1840s, congestion in the West End and City continued to increase and it became obvious that more needed to be done to alleviate the traffic problem. Even in the middle of the 19th century the traffic in London was so bad that it

was often quicker to walk between City destinations than take a cab or an omnibus. A whole series of redevelopments attempted to change this, including

channeling the remaining exposed sections of the Fleet River, now little more than an urban sewer; the construction of Shaftesbury Avenue in 1886; and the rebuilding of

Castle Street and Crown Street as the Charing Cross Road in 1887 to connect Trafalgar Square, Oxford Street and the Tottenham Court Road.

But the greatest scheme of the time was the construction of the Thames Embankments. Between 1867 and 1874, under the direction of the engineer, Sir Joseph Bazalgette (1819-1891), three major

The building of the railways had one other unexpected consequence: it led to the standardization of time throughout the United Kingdom. Until the production of railway timetables provided the necessity for standard time, each town and region of the Britain operated on its own local time. Between 1840 and 1850 most of the railway companies began to operate timetables using London Time. This became more common after 1852, when an hourly time signal was sent to railway stations by telegraph from the Royal Observatory at Greenwich. The use of different times still caused confusion. Some towns even fitted a second minute-hand to their clocks: one giving the local time, the other the London time. In 1880 Parliament finally passed an act to enforce London time, now called "British standard time," across the whole country. Pictured above is the interior of the clock tower at the Houses of Parliament, commonly called "Big Ben" although this strictly is the name of the huge clock bell in the tower. Pictured left is the magnetic clock at the Greenwich Observatory.

embankments along the Thames were constructed: the Victoria Embankment, the Albert Embankment and the Chelsea Embankment. It had been hoped that the embankment and its new roads would relieve the volume of traffic in Fleet Street and the Strand, but people were slow to use it, in 1874 it was reported that it was used only by "a few foreigners or country people, or hansoms [cabs] uncommonly knowing drivers," but that Fleet Street was "gorged, crowded from end to end."

Divisions of class

During the 18th century London's suburbs had become divided into wealthy districts such as Piccadilly and Mayfair and predominantly working-class areas such as Spitalfields in the East End.

By the 19th century, class and wealth were increasingly dividing London. William Birt, the General Manager of the Great Eastern Railway, probably expressed the feelings of many of the growing middle classes when he claimed that the presence of the working class and poor in Edmonton, Stratford and Walthamstow had made the areas "spoilt for ordinary residential purposes," and he argued for even greater segregation, saying that "districts which are not spoilt should not be thrown open to the working classes."

Bridge-building and rebuilding across the Thames reached something of a frenzy in the 19th century. London Bridge was one of the first for development, as shown in this contemporary sketch of the bridge's formal opening in 1831. Meanwhile, the 18th-century Blackfriars' Bridge was found to have been undermined at its foundations, and was replaced by the present bridge in 1860-69. Built by Joseph Cubitt, it was opened by Queen Victoria, who was so unpopular at the time that she was hissed by the crowds as she rode down the Strand in her carriage. Under the river, the Blackwall Tunnel was constructed, connecting Greenwich to the East India Dock. Constructed between 1891 and 1897 it was at the time the longest underwater tunnel in the world at 4,410 ft.

As areas became unfashionable, those with the economic power to do so moved out. As one commentator wrote in 1845, the middle classes "move either toward the west, or emigrate to the suburbs—the one for fashion, the other for economy and fresh air."

The development of the public transport system allowed them to move further from central London and away from their working-class neighbors. In a cyclical process as they moved to new areas, so the working classes moved into the districts they had vacated. As the middle classes populated new suburbs, so the transport network expanded to serve them. Better communications and cheaper fares encouraged this migration to the new suburbs. As the transport network improved, it allowed, for those who could afford it, to move into even more distant suburbs, and the whole process began again. Evidence of this can be seen in working-class suburbs all over London where splendid old houses hint at a genteel middle-class past.

Initially it was only the well-off and the upper middle classes who could afford to travel back and forth from the suburbs by train. A survey of 1854 showed that the

With the growth of the East End it was becoming obvious that London needed a crossing of the Thames downriver of London Bridge. Work started in 1884 on the new bridge. With two lifting roadways—each weighing 1,000 tons, to allow ships to enter the upper pool of London—built in "fairytale" Gothic, Tower Bridge is still one of the most famous symbols of London. Within a month of its completion the roadway had been opened 655 times; today with the decline of the traffic on the Thames, it opens about 500 times a year.

majority of commuters still walked to work: about 10,000 came by train, 15,000 by steamboat and 20,000 by omnibus and a further 200,000 walked. The Government, however, was keen to use the railways as a means to alleviate the chronic housing crisis that had been caused in part by the building of the railways themselves, and began to incorporate an obligation on the railways to provide cheap and convenient working men's trains as part of their permission to build.

The laying of the new routes into London involved the clearance of vast tracts of housing in the inner city. It did not take long for the railway companies to realize that it was far cheaper and easier to drive their lines through working-class districts where the property prices were lower and they would face less opposition. Although by the middle of the 19th century the railways and the developers had an obligation to rehouse those whose homes they demolished; they would often get around this by offering a few pounds compensation as a cheaper alternative.

LIFE AND LABOUR
OF THE PEOPLE
IN LONDON

EDITED BY
CHARLES BOOTH

VOLUME I
EAST, CENTRAL AND SOUTH LONDON

London
MACMILLAN AND CO.
AND NEW YORK
1889

Charles Booth, in his book, *Life and Labour of the People of London* (1889), divided those Londoners who were not part of the aristocracy and upper classes into eight groups. These eight groups ranged from Group A, the lowest class, who Booth considered to be "occasional laborers, street sellers, loafers, criminals and semi-criminals. Their life is the life of savages, with vicissitudes of extreme hardship and their only luxury is drink" to Group H, London's "upper-middle class, servant-keeping class". Groups A and B represented the very poor, Groups C and D were poor, and Groups E to H were all above the poverty line. Groups D or E included those people with small regular earnings (poor), or standard regular earnings (above the poverty line).

"Congregations of vice and misery"

The demolition of London's slum-housing was seen as a benefit. It was believed that driving wide roads through poor areas would introduce light and air to the residents, and the demolition of poor quality housing was another benefit since it destroyed "congregations of vice and misery."

However, although the overall population figures for the inner-city districts were falling, the density of occupation in these areas was increasing. Those who could leave did, but for the poor this was often not an option. Many workers still needed to be within walking distance of their employment, especially casual laborers or those who took in out-work such as weavers and some artisans like watchmakers who worked from home but needed to be within easy distance of their markets and retailers. The result was that instead of dispersing the population the demolition of the housing stock merely concentrated them in the buildings that remained.

In 1865 the Medical Officer for the Strand described the process, explaining that the poor "merely migrate to the nearest courts and streets and then provide themselves with homes, by converting the house up to this time occupied by a single family, into one tenanted by nearly as many families as the rooms it contains." This inability of the poor to move away when their homes were lost through redevelopment is illustrated by the construction of New Oxford Street in 1844-47. The construction of this road required the demolition of smaller roads and houses. As a result the population of nearby Church Lane, a small street of only 28 houses, increased from 655 in 1841 to a staggering 1,095 in 1847—the equivalent to 39 people per house.

One contemporary report revealed that in the lodging houses around Charing Cross, "shelter is obtained, with a bed of straw, for 2d to 4d per night, and where this is not obtainable, the arches under the Adelphi afford a shelter. In the lodging-rooms

What we would term today as "inner city decay" has always been a problem in London. "Rookeries" were deprived urban areas that had become built-up slums. One of the most notorious was Seven Dials, the area between St Giles's and Covent Garden, shown here in 1850 (note the free-roaming pig in the foreground), where even the police refused to go.

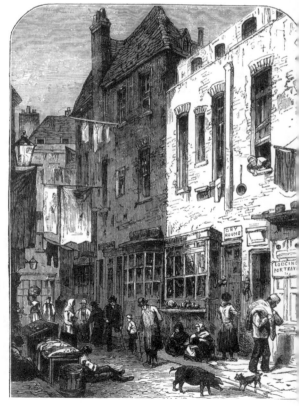

I have seen the beds placed so close together as not to allow room to pass between them, and occupied by both sexes indiscriminately. I have known six people sleep in a room about nine feet square, with only one small window, about 17 inches by 12 inches; and there are some sleeping rooms in this district in which you cannot scarcely see your hand at noonday."

As the inner-city districts like Whitechapel and Soho became crowded and began to degenerate into slums, called "rookeries," it was hardly surprising that those with the economic freedom to do so began to move out, especially when the inner city also became associated with epidemics and disease. The drains and sewers too were inadequate; while some parts of the City had good well maintained drains, most of the rest of London did not. Where they did exist drains and sewers were unreliable and often leaked, before dumping their contents directly into the Thames, turning the river into an open sewer where refuse and excrement would be washed up and down river by the tide.

The problem of the city's worsening water supply was summed up in no uncertain terms by Sydney Smith, the Canon of St. Paul's Cathedral. Writing in 1834 to a friend in a letter, he complained: "He who drinks a tumbler of London water has literally in his stomach more animated beings than there are men, women and children on the face of the globe." The contemporary cartoon was drawn in 1828 by the satirist William Heath, depicting the appalling state of the capital's drinking water. The caption reads: "Microscopia, or Monster Soup commonly called Thames Water, being a correct representation of that precious stuff doled out to us!"

Killers in the slums

In these conditions, ill health and death were commonplace, tuberculosis was prevalent until the 1870s and smallpox was another common killer. By the 1830s it was decreasing (and by 1898 had been virtually eradicated by an inoculation campaign) but it could nevertheless still occur in dangerous outbreaks; in 1840 an epidemic killed 6,400 Londoners and a further 14,000 Londoners perished in an outbreak in

1871-2. But the two great killers of the Victorian slums were typhus and cholera. Typhus is a very infectious bacterial disease spread by lice living in human feces. In the unsanitary conditions of the overcrowded rookeries, lice thrived. For ten years during the 1860s while London was undergoing its most intensive period of road and railway building, the disease was endemic in the London slums.

But it was cholera that was most feared. A group of residents from the rookery of St. Giles expressed their fears in a letter to *The Times* in 1848. Fifty-four residents signed the letter, which was published by the paper without any correction, which read: "Sur, may we beg and beseech your proteckshion and power... we live in muk and filthe. We aint got no privez [lavatories] no dust bins, no drains, no water splies [supplies]...if the colera comes Lord help us."

Like typhus, cholera was a bacterial disease but it was spread by contact with contaminated sewage, it could be passed by physical contact, by flies but most commonly by drinking water. Although cholera killed fewer people than typhus or influenza, it was feared because of its violence and virulence. Victims suffered from severe vomiting and diarrhea, with whole families dying within hours of the onset of the disease.

The Methodist Magazine said of it in 1832: "To see a number of fellow creatures, in a good state of health, in full possession of their wanton strength, and in the midst of their years, suddenly seized with the most violent spasms, and in a few hours cast into the tomb, is calculated to shake the firmest nerves, and to inspire dread in the stoutest hearts." When in 1831-32 the first of four cholera epidemics broke out in Great Britain, 31,000 people died, 5,000 of them in London.

Central London had 88 ancient churchyards, and in a normal year they would have to accommodate 18,000 corpses. Out of necessity, bodies were often buried only a few inches below the ground surface and were frequently disturbed by new internments. The cemeteries often stank and heavy rain could unearth the bodies, one woman complained that in St. Olave's Churchyard (pictured), she had seen four exposed putrefying heads. During epidemics the cemeteries were inundated and had difficulty coping, adding to the delays of disposing of the dead and prolonging the exposure of the living to infectious corpses.

Curing epidemics

It was becoming increasingly evident that something needed to be done about the unsanitary conditions of the Metropolis, but what? Until the 1880s the cause of the epidemics and how they were transmitted was not properly understood. The general consensus was that disease was spread through bad air, called "miasma." Miasma, it was believed, was caused by bad smells given off by accumulated rubbish and sewage. The social reformer Edwin Chadwick, representing the Poor Law Commission, argued that disease was a major cause of the poverty with which the Poor Law had to deal, that by increasing the health of the population one would decrease the demand for poor relief. In 1838 following an outbreak of typhus in East London, Chadwick instigated an inquiry into sanitary conditions and health in London that found "the causes of fever in the metropolis might be removed by proper sanitary measures."

Other cholera epidemics followed, and in 1854 an outbreak killed 10,738 Londoners. But this time there was a glimmer of hope. In 1849 it had been suggested that cholera was transmitted through

In the first half of the 19th century only the houses of the very wealthy had "water-closets" fitted; most houses still disposed of sewage in cesspits dug in the yard, or built directly under the house. Many landlords allowed the cesspits to fill to overflowing in order to sell the "night soil" as fertilizer. The cesspits were occasionally, and usually inefficiently, emptied by "night men" (above right) who, because of the lack of space in the cesspits and culverts would employ small children to do the cleaning. It was a dangerous and unhygienic job: the accumulated fumes alone could be deadly, causing almost instant death or asphyxiation. Another hazardous job was that of the rat-catchers (above left) who worked in the sewers.

polluted water. During this latest epidemic, Dr John Snow showed how the distribution of 500 cholera deaths in one part of Soho was related to the use of a specific water pump in Broad Street (now Broadwick Street).

This was reinforced by a survey of 500,000 Londoners published in 1856 by John Simon, he showed that deaths among the customers of the Southwark and Vauxhall Water Company who took their supplies from the Thames at Battersea were 130 per 10,000 during the 1854 outbreak, whereas for customers of the Lambeth Water Company, whose supply came from the non-tidal reaches of the Thames was only 37 per 10,000. In the 1848-49 epidemic, when the Lambeth Company also took its supplies from the Thames, the death rate had been about the same between the two companies. Simon in fact had been very successful in his attempts to clean up the City of London. His offensives against squalor and the slums, his work on street cleaning and

During the cholera epidemic of 1848-49, local authorities were pressed to empty cess pits, remove refuse and other nuisances as well as evacuate the healthy to safety. But many did nothing. In exasperation, *The Times* wrote in 1849: "The parochial officers did nothing—absolutely nothing. They left the graveyards festering—cess pools seething—the barrels of blood steaming in the underground shambles [slaughterhouse] —the great mounds of scutch putrefying in the Bermondsey glue yards." From July to October 1849 cholera killed 14,000 Londoners (above left is the funeral of victims). In an attempt to control the spread of the disease, the Metropolitan Sewers Commission organized the flushing of the city sewers into the Thames, ironically the worst thing it could have possibly done. The water pump (pictured below left) in Broadwick Street marks the focus of Dr. John Snow's pioneering study of the 1854 Soho cholera epidemic. Following his theory that polluted drinking water was the means of transmission of the disease, he mapped cholera deaths with the source of the victim's drinking water, leading to this pump.

maintenance for the sewers and the provision of water to the city from the new covered reservoirs of the New River Company saved many lives. Out of the 10,738 deaths in London during the 1854 epidemic, only 211 were in the City of London.

The Great Stink

But the debate over sanitation was still going when London suffered from the Great Stink in 1858. The summer of 1858 was hot and the smell of the untreated sewage in the Thames became overpowering. The smell from the river was so bad in the Houses of Parliament that the MPs were forced to leave the debating chamber and the functioning of parliament became almost impossible; in order to combat the smell the windows were hung with curtains soaked in chloride of lime and there was even talk of moving the law courts to Oxford. Benjamin Disraeli (1804-1881), the future prime minister, described the Thames as "a Stygian pool reeking with ineffable and unbearable horrors," and he immediately introduced a bill to assist the construction of a new sewer system.

So appalled were the MPs by their own experience that the bill was passed in just 16 days and provided £3,000,000 for the Metropolitan Board of Works (M.B.W.) to spend as it saw fit. Work was begun almost immediately on the new system. The Chief Engineer was Joseph Bazalgette. His scheme was to build sewers that would intercept all the previous sewers draining into the Thames and carry the sewage eastward, dumping it in the river further downstream where it would be carried out to sea by the tide. By 1865 the new system was fully operational, with over 82 miles of sewers laid and there were six steam-driven pumping stations, at a cost of £4.6 million. The new system dumped 52,000,000 gallons of rainwater and sewage into the Thames downstream at Erith and Becton, but was capable of handling a massive 420,000,000 gallons.

Edwin Chadwick (1800-1890) of the Poor Law Commission was a fanatical social reformer who believed in paternalistic state intervention to improve people's lives, particularly in health. In 1842 he privately published his *Report... on an Inquiry into the Sanitary Conditions of the Laboring Population.* The report became a bestseller, in which Chadwick called for the construction of proper sewers and provision of a good water supply in London. But he alienated many with a self-conviction that bordered on bullying arrogance. Nevertheless when he died, his obituary in *The Times* paid tribute, saying: "Had he killed in battle as many as he saved by sanitation, he would have had equestrian statues by the dozen put up to his memory!"

The water supply slowly improves

Unfortunately the improvements in the drainage of London could not prevent another outbreak of cholera in 1865-66, although it did lessen its impact. The last epidemic was worst in the deprived East End of London where the East London Water Company was still supplying water directly from the polluted River Lea, a major tributary of the Thames. In London 5,915 people died in the outbreak, of these 4,276 lived in the East End. Despite the record of the East London Water Company, London's water supply did slowly improve. By the end of the 1860s clean water was available from the water companies either through public pumps or piped directly into houses, with the result that by 1880 virtually all of London's public wells had been closed. A constant supply of water was a commonplace by 1900.

Part of the enduring problem of the Victorian Age was also the lack of affordable housing for the very poor, those who had only an irregular income or who Booth might describe as "occasional laborers, loafers and semi-criminals." Despite their attempts to do so the Victorians failed to find a way of providing decent housing for the very poor and the problem would not be properly addressed until the 20th century. Between 1855 and 1868 various Parliamentary Acts limited the numbers of people permitted in lodging houses and rented accommodation, and local authorities were enabled to close buildings that were overcrowded.

Despite the powers granted to them by Parliament local authorities were often reluctant to act. Based on their experience with slum clearance for roads and railways it was evident that closing down overcrowded housing would simply move the problem, and

Improvements in the sanitary condition of London were such that when another cholera epidemic affected Europe in 1892 there were no deaths in London. But London's poorer districts continued to have higher mortality rates than those of London's wealthier boroughs. During the 1890s babies born in Limehouse, Shoreditch, and Southwark had a one in five chance of dying before their first birthday, whereas for babies born in the more affluent area of Hampstead the figure was one in ten. Pictured below is a lodging house showing the insanitary, crowded conditions in which many people in the city lived. Note the open sewer running under the building.

create greater population densities in nearby accommodation. In 1875 the Artisans' and Laborers' Dwellings Act was passed. The new legislation empowered the City Sewer Commissioners and the M.B.W. to demolish areas of slum housing and sell the land to build new housing, as long as the

number of new dwellings was equal to the number of dwellings demolished. The cleared land would be sold to one of the many housing charities, these were in fact companies, who combined the opportunity to gain a modest, five percent, return on an invested sum, with the Victorians' strong sense of charitable paternalism.

The Peabody Trust

Perhaps the most famous of the new housing trusts was the Peabody Trust, founded by the American philanthropist and businessman George Peabody (1795-1869). A regular traveler to England for business, he finally settled in London in 1837 where he became a wealthy and successful merchant banker.

His interest in the London Poor was aroused by Lord Shaftesbury, a social reformer and supporter of Edwin Chadwick;, as a result Peabody donated £500,000 to "to ameliorate the condition of the poor and needy of this great metropolis and to promote their comfort and happiness." The Trust's activities were to be directed toward the poor "in the ordinary sense of the word." Peabody's original foundation was not specifically directed toward housing but to general

Adding to London's unpleasantness was the old Smithfield Market. This had been the main livestock market in the City since the Middle Ages. During the 19th century, the number of animals passing through the market was vast: in 1846 alone 210,000 head of cattle and 1,518,000 sheep were brought to the market. The animals were brought in on the hoof, herded through the streets leaving them, in the words of Charles Dickens, "nearly ankle-deep with filth and mire." The animals at Smithfield were sold and then killed in local abattoirs, often domestic houses with the refuse simply thrown into the streets outside.

assistance of the poor; it was his trustees who decided that part of the money should be put toward the construction of "cheap, cleanly, well drained and healthful dwellings for the poor."

Despite living in England Peabody maintained his links to the United States where he founded several educational and philanthropic institutions in New England. In 1869 he was given the "Freedom" of the City of London, the first United States citizen to be given that honor. (To this day there have been only two: the other was Dwight D. Eisenhower.)

Nevertheless all the housing companies and trusts, including Peabody's, were relatively expensive and drew their tenants not from the poorest inhabitants of the slums but from the better off artisans, skilled workers and laborers who enjoyed a regular income. The companies encouraged this with the provision of rules and regulations that deterred many of the poorest. The supervisors would not allow anyone they considered to be "drunkards, brawlers, prostitutes," or those with immoral habits to take up residence. The aim was to lift up respectable families from the inequity of their surroundings, and remove them from the harmful influence of the very poor. As one poor old lady told the Royal Commission on the Housing of the Working Classes in 1885: "I came to London 25 years ago, and I've never lived in any room for more than two years yet. They always say they want to pull down the house to build dwellings for poor people, but I've never got into one yet."

Lure of the suburbs

For those with the economic or occupational freedom to do so, moving to the suburbs was an increasingly popular option during the Victorian period. In

The American merchant banker George Peabody led an eventful and profitable life. He was born in Danvers, Massachusetts, in 1795. His parents were relatively poor, and after only four years of formal education he was apprenticed to a local grocer. He fought against the British as a volunteer in the war of 1812. In London, Peabody mixed with the highest society and his Fourth of July dinners were famous. He died in 1869, and a funeral service was held in Westminster Abbey, where his body was temporarily buried. Peabody remains the only American to have been buried in Westminster Abbey. His body was returned to the U.S. on the British warship HMS Monarch, escorted by French and American warships. The illustration shows the Prince of Wales unveiling a statue of Peabody at the Royal Exchange.

marked contrast to the cramped and polluted conditions of the inner London districts, the suburbs offered those who could afford it clean air, privacy and space. By 1900 the suburbs had expanded to form a ring six miles deep around the City. It was the largest urban area in the world, and by the turn of the 20th century, housed one-fifth of the population of England and Wales.

The majority of the suburbs were centered on ancient villages that had been swallowed up by London's urban sprawl. At their heart was usually an ancient "high street" and church (many are still evident to this day), where local shops, solicitors, doctors, and schools would cater to the immediate needs of the suburban Londoner and his family. As one contemporary observer wrote: "Thus every district becomes sufficient for itself, industries of many kinds are started, the rural suburb becomes a busy and crowded town, with the peculiarity that the streets in the daytime are filled with women and children; and fortunes are made in local trade or in local speculation. The ladies are not obliged to go to Regent Street and Bond Street for the newest fashions and the most costly materials, for they can find these things on the spot."

The same commentator describes how the suburbs also offer social diversions: "The young men and lads

Because George Peabody had established his housing trust as an act of individual philanthropy, it had no need to pay dividends to shareholders and as a result could charge cheaper rent than the "five percent companies" working in the provision of affordable housing at the time. This ability of the Peabody Trust to offer lower rents was attacked by the other companies, who claimed that it allowed tenants to take advantage of a competitive marketplace and prevented the other companies from raising their rents or generating enough income to carry out improvements to their housing stock. By the 1890s, the Peabody Trust had built 5,000 dwellings and housed 20,000 people. Despite all their problems, the housing charities did provide good, clean, and healthy accommodation for a great many Londoners, and it has been calculated that by 1891 four percent of all Londoners lived in philanthropic accommodation. Adding to these achievements, between 1890 and 1914, the L.C.C. cleared 58 acres of slums and replaced them with blocks of two or three-bedroom flats.

The fields that once separated villages such as Hammersmith, Ealing, Hampstead, New Cross, Deptford, or Lewisham from London had by 1900 become solid networks of roads and houses, usually centered on a new church, often built in the Gothic style. But even the suburbs were distinguishable by their residents: Dalston, Brixton, New Cross, Forest Hill, Walthamstow and Tottenham were the suburbs of clerks. Kennington, Stockwell, and Camberwell housed City tradesmen. The "richer sort" inhabited Balham, Sydenham, Highgate, Hampstead, Barnes, and Richmond.

have their bicycle clubs, their ramblers' clubs, their football, cricket, rowing clubs; they have their institutes and polytechnics, where there are libraries, gymnasia, debating societies, chess clubs; they have orchestral and choral societies, lectures, concerts and even dances. The girls who have been brought up under these influences are less frivolous, much healthier; they know a great deal more; they take broader views of life; they are even taller and stronger."

Boom in the city's stores

It is easy to see London in the time of Victoria as a city of inner slums and outer suburbs. Certainly the growth of the suburbs was remarkable, but even this expansion would be overshadowed by the suburban growth of the 20th century, and the slums, although terrible and unpleasant, were confined to specific parts of the city. Despite everything, Victorian London was a rich, imperial, commercial and trading city, and the Victorians reflected this status in their buildings. Large banks and offices, built in the Italian Renaissance style, began to replace the small domestic houses of the City and it has been calculated that four out of every five of the buildings standing in 1855 were rebuilt by 1900.

In addition there was a boom in the number

of shops in London. In the suburbs many small houses built single flat roof extensions out over their front gardens to provide shops, but the 19th century also saw the rise of the chain store. The firm of J. Sainsbury had started as Drury Lane dairy in 1869 but expanded during the 1880s and by 1914 had 115 grocery stores throughout London. By 1916 both Marks & Spencer and Woolworth had dozens of stores throughout London.

Other shops were expanding into department stores. On Oxford Street, Peter Robinson, linen Draper had expanded from a single shop in 1833 into the five adjacent properties by 1860. Other familiar department stores included John Lewis, Heals, Maples, Fenwicks, Army & Navy, Swan & Edgar, Dickens & Jones . . . the list goes on. Whiteley's department store was described in 1887 as "an immense symposium of the arts and industries of the nation and of the world," and by 1906 it had 159 different departments. Harrods built its current store in the Brompton Road in 1897-1905, and Harry G. Selfridge opened his grand department store in 1909. By 1914 Selfridges alone employed 950 men and 2,550 women in 160 departments.

There was also a growing number of outlets for recreation. Trips to the coast remained a popular day out, or to one of the suburban green spaces like Richmond, Blackheath, or Hampstead Heath, or one of the many new open spaces like Victoria Park in Hackney opened in 1845 or the 3,000 acres of Epping Forest saved from development in 1874 and opened to the public in 1882.

Above: Heraldic cast-iron panels by Joseph Armitage on the front of the Heal's building in Tottenham Court Road designed by Cecil Brewer in 1916. Heal's philosophy has always been to imbue its stylish furniture and fittings with a human, practical spirit.
Below: Shopfront of the first Marks & Spencer "bazaar" in Holloway, 1914. The company swiftly expanded across the United Kingdom to become the nation's most high-profile department store.

Londoners also enjoyed sports. Soccer (called football in Britain) was the most popular game to play and watch. Formal rules were

introduced in the 1860s and teams would be organized by workers, churches, pubs. Eight London Clubs took place in the first Football Association (FA) Cup in 1871-72 and by 1883-84 there were 21 London teams involved. By 1908 five London Clubs were playing in the Football League, Arsenal (the oldest of the London soccer clubs), Leyton Orient, Chelsea, Fulham, and Tottenham Hotspur. Crowds of between 10,000 and 50,000 people were common at London soccer matches during the 1890s. Both watching and playing soccer was always a largely working-class recreation, for the middle classes there was always tennis or golf, while the game of cricket was swiftly gaining popularity among those of all backgrounds.

Barry and Pugin's new Houses of Parliament

London's position as a national and imperial capital was displayed in the city's public buildings. These included the rebuilding of the Royal Exchange and the relocation of the Royal Courts of Justice. The ancient Palace of Westminster had been destroyed by fire in 1834: only Westminster Hall, the cloisters and the undercroft of St. Stephens Chapel had survived. To find a design for a replacement, Parliament held a competition; their only specification was that the building had to be in either the Gothic or the Elizabethan style. It was felt that these two styles were particularly British and were therefore the only styles

A wave of public building included social facilities such as bathhouses, schools, libraries, and museums. The British Museum was rebuilt in 1852, there were private shows and exhibitions too, like Madam Tussaud's Waxworks, opened in 1835. The "Great Globe" in Leicester Square opened in 1851—40ft in diameter and 60ft high, it had a relief map of the world on a scale of one inch to ten miles sculpted onto its interior. The public could view the map from a series of galleries and staircases. There were also various display rooms containing maps, globes and atlases. The Globe was a great attraction until its sale and demolition in 1862.

suitable for the home of the British Parliament.

The competition was won by the architect Charles Barry in collaboration with the designer Augustus Pugin, who was responsible for the internal and external decoration. Barry initially estimated that the work would take six years at a cost of £80,000. But he had to make so many alterations to his original scheme that in the end it took about 30 years and cost over £2,000,000. It was widely believed that the strain drove Barry to an early death in 1860, seven years before the building was completed. His son completed the task. Constructed between 1837 and 1867 in orange-brown limestone with a multitude of turrets and pinnacles, the building's 316-foot-high clock tower has become one of the

After fire razed the Houses of Parliament in 1834, they were rebuilt in grand style. The clock tower and clock of the Houses of Parliament are known as Big Ben, although this is really the name of the bell that rings the hour. The original bell weighed 16 tons and was cast in Stockton-on-Tees, but it cracked during tests. The second bell was cast in Whitechapel, and was hauled up the clock tower on its side. This bell also cracked but it was never replaced.

enduring symbols of London. In 1987 Barry's legacy was recognized by UNESCO as "an eminent example, coherent and complete, of the neo-Gothic style," and was inscribed on their list of World Heritage Sites.

The Royal Courts of Justice, which had sat in Westminster since the Middle Ages, were rehoused in a new, larger building. In 1865 the government provided £1,453,000 to purchase land on the Strand for the new building. The site was a notorious slum whose clearance was seen as beneficial to the general good. The Royal Courts of Justice are built of brick, faced with Portland stone in a "fairytale" Gothic design. There are 3.5 miles of corridors and more than 1,000 rooms. Its centerpiece is the great vaulted Gothic hall, and is one of London's finest interiors.

Electricity and telephones

It was not just new buildings that were changing the appearance of London or the habits of Londoners. The introduction of electric lighting at the end of the century literally put more hours in the day, and the coming of the telephone connected London to the rest of the country and the world to an extent that the telegraph had never achieved. Street lighting was not new to Victorian London, gaslights had been introduced into the city in the early 19th century, but by the 1880s they began to give way to brighter and more efficient electric lights.

The American engineer Thomas Edison (1847-1931) established a power station in the basement at the Holborn Viaduct in 1881-82 to supply the Old Bailey and the General Post Office. In 1885 the Grosvenor Art Gallery, Bond Street, became London's first unlikely commercial power station. When the owner installed electric lighting, he found that his generator had excess capacity and so he began to supply power to local shopkeepers. This eventually

became the London Electric Supply Corporation.

By 1900 London had over 200 miles of street illuminated by electricity. It had become the preferred means of lighting factories, hotels, large warehouses, railway terminals, trains and the homes of the rich. There were 15 electric companies with 30 power stations in London.

At the same time electricity was being installed in London, so was the newly invented telephone. The first London telephone exchange opened in Coleman Street in 1879 with only a handful of subscribers. Within two years the system had grown to just under 1,000 subscribers and 50 exchanges in London. As it expanded it became possible to call other cities in the country. In 1891, the first submarine telephone cable was laid to connect the telephone line between London and Paris, and by 1892 it was possible to phone Marseilles, Brussels, Belfast or Dublin from London.

The Great Exhibition

London in the 19th century was the largest, the richest as well as the greatest commercial and trading city in the world. It contained the palaces and houses of the British aristocracy and the monarchy, and it was the center of government not just for Great Britain but also for the British Empire, the greatest empire the world had ever known and over which, the British proudly claimed, the sun never set.

It was against this background that Prince Albert, Queen Victoria's husband, gave his support to the world's first international exhibition: the "Great Exhibition of the Works of Industry of All Nations." It was staged in London in 1851 and, as Albert said, "a whole world of nature and art collected at the call of

Electricity revolutionized London, attracting pioneers from all over the world, eager to demonstrate and market their inventions for using the new power source. The American Thomas Edison set up his first power companies in the capital to supply lighting and the Italian Guglielmo Marconi, known as the father of radio, successfully demonstrated the transmission of wireless signals in London and on Salisbury Plain in the 1890s.

From this site
GUGLIELMO
MARCONI
made the first
public transmission
of wireless signals
on 27 July 1896

the Queen of Cities." The exhibition was staged in Hyde Park in a specially commissioned glass building designed by Joseph Paxton. The cutom-designed building was like something from a fairy tale. Although *The Times* called it a

"monstrous greenhouse," Queen Victoria described it as "one of the wonders of the worlds which we English may be proud of," and the building soon became known as the Crystal Palace.

The exhibits came from all over the world, including artillery pieces sent by Krupp of Germany and threshing machines from the United States. Some exhibits were exotic like the Koh-i-Noor diamond from India, displayed in a special cage and now incorporated into the English Crown Jewels. Others were unusual or eccentric, like the model of a floating church from Philadelphia for the use of seamen, or the "silent alarum bedstead" that pushed the sleeper out of bed and into a cold bath at a given hour to wake him up. Queen Victoria was particularly taken by a group of stuffed cats seated on chairs and posed as if drinking tea. Medals and prizes were awarded to those judged the best. In the five months that the exhibition was open it had six million visitors from all over the world. Special excursion trains were run into London from other parts of Britain and the South Eastern Railway ran a special daily cross-channel service into London from France.

The organizers of the Great Exhibition used some

Above, Queen Victoria opens the Great Exhibition of 1851, celebrating the economic might of the British Empire, in the specially built Crystal Palace in Hyde Park. It was planned to demolish the Crystal Palace at the end of the Exhibition. However, the building was purchased by the Brighton Railway Company and carefully dismantled and moved to a green-field site near Sydenham in South London—the area is still known today as Crystal Palace. The Palace survived as an exhibition venue until 1936 when it was destroyed by fire. Covering 19 acres, the vast building was constructed of glass panels (900,000 square feet of glass was used) on a pre-fabricated iron frame.

of their profits to purchase 87 acres of land in South Kensington, across the road from the site of the Crystal Palace. Here they proposed to build schools, colleges, museums, and concert halls. The brainchild of Prince Albert, "Museumland" was intended to educate and instruct through "the influence of Science and Art upon Productive Industry." The area is now home to an impressive collection of public institutions, including the Science Museum, the Victoria and Albert Museum, the Natural History Museum, as well as the Royal Albert Hall, the Imperial College of Science and Technology, and the Royal College of Music.

Constant struggle of the poor

For many Victorians there was an increasing sense of outrage and guilt that in such an age of Empire and progress, and amidst the vast wealth of Westminster and the City, there should be such a high degree of poverty among some sections of the population. But who made up the population? By 1851 London had a workforce of 1,115,000 people, approximately 13.75 percent of the entire workforce of England and Wales. In London there worked about 25 percent of the country's retail and wholesale dealers, government employees, as well as professionals and transport workers; 40 percent of the nation's banking, insurance and law workers; and 67 percent of those who worked in industries related to entertainment, art, literature and science. London also had 22 percent of the country's domestic servants. Only one-fifth of the working population was middle- or upper-class. The remainder stretched down the social scale from skilled and prosperous artisans to unskilled casual laborers. About two-thirds of the London workforce was involved in various service industries, giving rise to comments that London was a "city of shopkeepers and clerks."

For the majority of London's workers, living conditions were extremely poor. Most workers passed through periods of relative comfort and occasional poverty. Food accounted for between half

Prince Albert died in December 1861 of typhoid fever contracted from the drains at Windsor Castle. Queen Victoria continued to wear black in his memory until her death 40 years later. The Albert Memorial was raised to honor him. Completed in 1872, the monument was placed in Kensington Gardens overlooking South Kensington's "Museumland" that Albert had done so much to create.
Overleaf: The Crystal Palace and surrounding gardens in South London.

C J Bromley. Sc

and three quarters of a Londoner's earnings but the diet was often poor consisting mainly of bread and potatoes, and, when affordable, meat, usually bacon or pork and, for the very poor, offal. For London's middle and upper classes this was a strange world but one that was becoming increasingly presented to the middle classes by novelists such as Charles Dickens or through the works of a few intrepid reformers.

One of the most famous was the journalist, writer

and playwright Henry Mayhew (1812-1887). In the 1840s, he began a series of articles, published in the form of letters in *The Morning Chronicle* newspaper, which were subsequently published in 1851-62 as *London Labor and the London Poor*. Mayhew, who regarded poverty as a metropolitan-wide phenomenon, described the day-to-day life of some of London's poorest inhabitants, highlighting their constant struggle with starvation, ignorance and disease.

In 1861 *The Morning Post* newspaper published a series of articles entitled "Horrible London," by the journalist, John Hollingshead (1827-1904), who later published them in his ground-breaking book *Ragged London* in 1861. This was a door-to-door investigation of the living and working conditions of Londoners. Hollingshead concluded that at least a third of all Londoners lived in poverty. It was the East End that gained the worst reputation for poverty and crime.

This area with its docks and immigrant

London had 13.5 percent of the country's manufacturing workforce in the 1850s, although many of these trades declined in the second half of the century due to industrial competition from elsewhere. There were 373,000 manufacturing workers, the clothing industry employed about 28,000 men and 84,000 women, there were a further 1,7000 women involved in the textile industry, 7,000 in shoe and boot-making and 8,000 had occupations related to the trade in fur, hair, paper, furniture, jam or baking. The manufacturing workforce included 30,000 shoe and boot-makers, 33,000 in woodwork and furniture, 23,000 in the metal trades, 14,000 in printing and book binding, 10,000 in fur, leather, glue and tallow, 9,000 watch and instrument makers, 9,000 carriage and harness makers, 7,000 in drink, and 6,000 in jewelry-making. Many more thousands were employed in shipbuilding, but the industry on the Thames eventually collapsed. Not all industry came from the trades, however. Some came from use of the poor in workhouses, such as these stone-breakers in Bethnal Green.

population, where the favors of a prostitute could be found for the price of a glass of gin, both fascinated and repelled the Victorian middle class. It was widely believed that the East End was an area of racial, moral and sexual danger where opium dens, boarding houses and alcohol encouraged immorality and disease among a population who were described as "savage, unclean and irreclaimable."

Jack the Ripper

The East End was the setting for one of history's most notorious serial killers. The Whitechapel Murders are perhaps better known today as the Jack the Ripper Killings. Between August and November 1888 the Ripper killed at least five, and perhaps more, women, all of whom were either active or part-time prostitutes. The Ripper either killed or rendered his victims unconscious through strangulation before he slashed and mutilated them with a knife.

The newspapers ran with the story and there was a great deal of fear in the East End. The streets were

quiet at night and there was a widespread feeling that the police were doing little to catch the murderer, who it was believed was either a foreigner or a Jew. Some local residents, including several Jews eager to act positively to stem the growing anti-Semitism the case was causing, formed the Mile End Vigilance Committee.

Jack the Ripper was never caught and his identity remains unknown to this day

The writer and journalist Charles Dickens was born in 1812 in Portsmouth and moved to London as a child. The poverty and adversity his family suffered contributed greatly to his later views on social reform in a country in the throes of the Industrial Revolution, as well as his compassion for the lower classes, especially children. After his death in 1870, he was buried in Poet's Corner, Westminster Abbey, where the inscription on his tombstone reads: "He was a sympathiser to the poor, the suffering, and the oppressed; and by his death, one of England's greatest writers is lost to the world. The stories, characters, and places he wrote about will live forever."

Left: A contemporary newspaper picture showing Jack the Ripper as he is invited into a house in the East End by one of his unsuspecting victims.

although there are several "suspects" and he is still as notorious today as he was in 1888. There are many different theories about his identity. It has even been claimed that there have been more books written about Jack the Ripper than all of the U.S. presidents combined. Jack got his name from two letters taunting the police that were sent to a news agency, written in red ink. They were signed "Jack the Ripper," the name stuck, even though it is not known if the letters were authentic. A third letter, but in a different handwriting, and a portion of human kidney were sent to George Lusk of the Mile End Vigilance Committee.

Horror of the workhouses

Despite the East End's reputation, it was not London's only concentration of slums, nor was it actually London's worst. Virtually every district in the city had its slum and poor areas, with South London suburbs being perhaps the worst. Having identified the poorest areas of London, middle-class Victorian opinion was divided about what to do about it. As well as the Poor Law that provided assistance for the destitute in prison-like workhouses, there was, in the early years of Victoria's reign, a belief in charity, through alms giving, emergency relief and education.

However there was a growing feeling among the middle classes that charity merely allowed "clever and lazy paupers" to get rich on handouts. Increasingly it was felt that the poor should be forced to rely on the Poor Law provisions of the workhouse. But the regime in these institutions was so horrific that many of the poor preferred hunger and destitution. In

Workhouse is a word that often conjures up the harsh and squalid world of Oliver Twist. The workhouse could be a grim and brutal place, where the poor lived and worked in buildings that were run in a similar way to prisons. Various acts of Parliament allowed parishes to club together into unions responsible for building workhouses and for running them. Hundreds of workhouses were built at a typical cost to the union of £5,000. By 1926, in Britain there were 226,000 inmates & around 600 workhouses with an average population of about 400 inmates each. Both working and living conditions in London were terrible for much of the population and riots were as commonplace as they had always been. Below is a scene of the police quelling a street disturbance in 1844.

1869 the Charity Organization Society (C.O.S.) was formed with the aim of coordinating charity work and prevent exploitation. The C.O.S. hoped that by strictly controlling charity it could direct the poor through the workhouse system, and encourage the poor to become self-reliant, to help them to help themselves. The C.O.S. believed that many of the problems could be solved by getting the well off to move back to poor areas from the suburbs, where they could lead by example and administer both politics and charity.

This led to the formation of the University Settlement movement in the 1880s to educate and provide teaching and recreation for the poor. "Settlers" included William Beveridge, Clement Attlee and R. H. Tawney, men who later went on to become highly influential politicians. The Settlement Movement led directly to the building of the Whitechapel Art Gallery in 1897-99 and the creation of the Workers Educational Association (W.E.A.) in 1903 to promote higher education among working men.

There was also a long tradition of the Church sending missions into the slums and the inter-denominational London City Mission was founded in 1835. The Church of England sent several Anglican missions into London, and Anglican clergymen were instrumental in the formation of "Ragged Schools" and the development of Christian Socialism.

Rioting in the streets

There was political agitation in London too. In the 1880s the formation of trade unions and of Marxist and socialist organizations began to worry the middle and upper classes. There had been working-class political movements before: in 1836 William Lovett had founded the London Working Man's Association, which had produced a People's Charter in 1838 calling for annual Parliaments, elected by universal male suffrage and the secret ballot.

Evangelical Christianity was very popular and successful in reviving working-class Christianity, forging close links with the evangelical movement in the United States. Foremost among its preachers was C. H. Spurgeon who regularly preached to crowds of 10,000, and in 1857 he drew a crowd of 23,654 at the Crystal Palace. The Catholic Church was also active, and had a large following especially among European immigrants and London's Irish community. Catholic parish churches and schools were built as well as two major Roman Catholic churches in London: Westminster Cathedral (pictured, begun 1884, opened 1903) in the Byzantine style, and the Brompton Oratory (1878-84) in the Italian Baroque style.

When the Charter was presented to Parliament in 1839, it had over a million signatures. Known as the Chartists the movement eventually collapsed through lack of strong leadership. The idea had not entirely died, however, and the first International Working Man's Association had been founded in London in 1864. But the movements of the 1880s had a new militancy about them. The winter of 1885-86 was the coldest for 30 years, and there was unemployment and unrest among the poor. On February 8 1886, a rally of about 20,000 unemployed dockers and builders held in Trafalgar Square exploded into a riot through the genteel streets of the neighboring areas of Mayfair and St. James.

More unrest followed: in November 1887, a rally of 100,000 marched from Clerkenwell to Trafalgar Square. Four thousand police had gathered to prevent them. When police baton charges failed to disperse the crowd, cavalry and guards with fixed bayonets were called out. Two civilians were killed and the event, known as Bloody Sunday, became a cornerstone of the British Socialist movement.

This agitation was followed by a series of strikes. The result of this new militancy was a breakdown of

While existing docks such as St. Katherine's (pictured above, by the Tower) were refitted, new docks were created further downstream to take the larger ships needed for the increased volume of world trade passing through London: the Royal Victoria Dock was built in 1855, Millwall Dock in 1868, and the Royal Albert Dock in 1880. There were warehouses, hotels (especially around the railway terminals) and market buildings. In the City, Smithfield Market (1866-67), Billingsgate Market (1874-78) and Leadenhall Market (1880-81) were all rebuilt by the Corporation, and the fruit and vegetable market at Covent Garden was expanded.

the C.O.S.'s charitable restrictions and a flood of charity toward the poor. There was a noted softening in the attitude of workhouses, especially toward the old. The growth of political awareness among the London working classes, especially through the work of organizations like the trade unions, the W.E.A. and the Fabian Society, founded in 1881 to promote socialist reform through constitutional agitation, led in 1892 to the election of the first Independent Labour Member of Parliament, Kier Hardie, the member of Parliament for West Ham. Hardie went on to become a co-founder and leader of the modern British Labour Party in 1906, which would in 1922 replace the Liberals as Britain's second major political party.

The Pax Britannica

The 20th century was less than a month old when on January 22, 1901, Queen Victoria died, and London as well as the whole country was plunged into mourning. The new monarch was the 60-year-old Prince of Wales, King Edward VII. In the 64 years of Queen Victoria's reign London had changed dramatically: the Victorian could see progress in every corner of the city, slums were being cleared, the poor rehoused, andschools provided free elementary education for all. Trains, trams and omnibuses traversed the city allowing people to move into the clean air of the suburbs, and in the last few decades of the reign the motorcar was first seen on the London streets. London was a rich and proud city basking in the wealth and peace of the British Empire's strength of arms—the "Pax Britannica."

So London entered the 20th century with a new King but with old certainties. Little were Londoners to know that in the space of a single lifetime London would be laid waste in a war on a scale that the Victorians could not even contemplate, and that the Empire would be gone along with Victorian certainty.

Although "Medieval Gothic" became the dominant architectural form of the Victorians, some architects did build in other styles. There was a revival of the Queen Anne style in the 1860s and 1870s. At Bedford Park, Turnham Green, built between 1875 and 1881 as a "Garden Suburb," the architect Norman Shaw designed the houses in the "Old English" style. This "Arts and Crafts" approach was influential in the 20th century and gave rise to the old English, mock-Tudor suburban house of the following century. Below is St. Paul's Studios, a row of custom-designed artists' houses in Barons Court, west London. Each has special studio rooms and large, south-facing windows to let in as much light as possible throughout the day.

CHAPTER 9
TRIUMPH AND TRANSITION

MODERN LONDON 1901 TO THE 21st CENTURY

"Yet despite its harrowing ordeal of the last seven years, London still marches on."
—Harold P. Clunn, *London Marches On* (1947)

"The aristocracy is in decline in the City, and the cloth-cap professionals are in the ascent. And we will take over."
—Paul Neild, Managing Director, Phillips & Drew, London, in "On the Aggressive New Breed in London's Financial District," *New York Times* (September 25, 1986)

Queen Elizabeth II presided over more than half a century of phenomenal change to both London and the United Kingdom that easily rivals the reigns of those other great rulers Elizabeth I and Victoria.

I N THE FIRST YEARS of the 20th century it must have appeared to many Londoners that the Age of Victoria had given way to an age of peace, progress and prosperity. As the politician Joseph Chamberlain (1836-1914) said in a speech at the London Guildhall in 1904,

"providing that the City of London remains, as it is at present, the clearing house of the world, any other nation may be its workshop," and there was no reason to believe that things would change. British military might had emerged victorious from the second Boer War (1899-1902) in South Africa, and despite occasional scare stories in the newspapers about the other European powers, these countries seemed to pose little real threat—and in any case, Britain, Russia and Germany were united by ties of blood, since Edward VII (1901-1910) was the uncle of the German kaiser and the Russian tsar.

Across the Atlantic, the United States was remote, a source of trade and emigration, but a country that seemed introverted and without any imperial ambitions. In 1901 the British Empire was still the greatest Empire the world had ever seen, and London was its capital, the largest and richest city on earth. The evidence of this new age of progress could be seen by Londoners in the technological advances that allowed the electrification of the city's railways and tram lines and the introduction to the city's streets of the motorbus, as well as in grand building schemes introducing a new and imposing architectural style.

From the last decade of the 19th century until the Depression of the 1930s, London was rebuilt on a physical scale unthinkable to the Victorians. This was made possible by building techniques that had been

One of the first public buildings erected in London in the new Baroque style was the Central Criminal Court, known as the Old Bailey and built (1900-07) on the site of

the demolished Newgate Prison. With its dome, columns, rusticated ground floor stonework and splendid sculptures it was an influential piece of monumental building.

pioneered in the United States and Continental Europe, such as the use of steel frames and reinforced concrete. The introduction of the elevator allowed buildings to be bigger and taller, and the introduction of electric lighting freed buildings from a reliance on large windows and skylights, allowing them to become much deeper than they had ever been before.

The style adopted for virtually all major buildings in this period was a revival of the English Baroque, which was thought to have a particularly unique Englishness suitable for the epicenter of the Empire. At the time, architects called it the English Renaissance Style. This has come to be known as Edwardian Baroque. Buildings erected in this style had massive frontages, domes, columns, towers and extravagant sculpture. Some of the buildings were on a giant scale with emphasized architectural features, especially on buildings erected after the First World War, in a style termed the "Grand Manner."

The Underground develops

The new building techniques transformed the face of London and new technology in the form of electric power and the gasoline engine was about to revolutionize London's public transportation system. In 1890 electricity had been used to power the three miles of underground railway belonging to the City and South London Railway between King William Street and Stockwell, a line known to Londoners as "The Tube." But for all their innovations, these lines were struggling to compete with the omnibuses and trams running the route above ground.

Another electric railway was the Waterloo and City Line, known to Londoners as "The Drain," between Waterloo Station and Bank, constructed 1894-98. In 1900 an Anglo-American syndicate

West of the City, the Mall was given a new layout between 1901 and 1913, with Admiralty Arch built in 1908-9 for the Navy at the junction of the Mall and Trafalgar Square, even the king followed suit, ordering a grand facade for Buckingham Palace in new Baroque style (1912-3). At the Aldwych, built by the L.C.C. between 1900 and 1905, the new buildings were large and impressive in the Grand Manner and the style was used equally for shops, banks, museums, stations, town halls, government buildings and offices, including County Hall the new L.C.C. offices on the south bank of the Thames opposite the Houses of Parliament between 1908 and 1922.

opened the Central London Railway. This was London's first deep-level electric railway, running from the City to the West End with stops that included the shopping centers of Oxford Street and Bayswater Road. The new line was an immediate success and soon was carrying 41 million passengers a year.

The older subway companies, the Metropolitan Line and the District Line, had trouble keeping up with the new technology. Both were still using steam power for their trains in the months following the opening of the Central London Railway. The two older companies lost four million passengers between them. Then in 1901 a flamboyant American financier and developer, Charles Tyson Yerkes, appeared on the London transportation scene. In 1902 at the head of a syndicate of Boston and New York financiers, he formed the Underground Electric Railways Company of London (U.E.R.L.), and started the modernization and expansion of the underground railway network. By 1905 the whole U.E.R.L. system was running electric trains powered by a new power station built by Yerkes at Lots Road, Chelsea.

Between 1906 and 1907, the U.E.R.L. opened three entirely new underground lines: the Bakerloo Line (1906), the Piccadilly Line (1906), and the Northern Line (1907). The Metropolitan Line remained independent of the U.E.R.L., but achieved full electrification early in 1905. Although when Yerkes died in 1905, the U.E.R.L. was close to bankruptcy, for Londoners his legacy was nevertheless an extensive and modern underground railway system.

Charles Tyson Yerkes was born in Philadelphia in 1837, and began his career as a humble clerk. After becoming a broker, by 1862 he had his own banking house. In 1871, he served seven months in prison for misappropriation of funds. But after his release and pardon, he regained his fortune. In 1882, he moved to Chicago and in four years had gained control of the city's public transportation system, which he developed and modernized. At the turn of the 20th century Yerkes sold his interest in the Chicago transportation system and moved to London to transform its own transportation system.

Electric trams and motorbuses

One of the reasons why the new Underground network failed to attract as many

passengers as had been estimated was the introduction of new technology to the above-ground transportation systems of London. First was the introduction of electric trams in 1901, replacing the old horse-drawn types. The omnibus was re-invented as the "motorbus." The capital's

first gasoline engine motorbus route was opened in 1899. These motorbuses were small vehicles run by operators who often lacked the financial resources to develop their services. In 1904 Tillings of Peckham invested in a fleet of 25 Daimler motorbuses to operate out of Oxford Circus. Although Tillings's motorbuses cost more to buy than an omnibus, they carried more passengers, they could cover more miles in a single day and had no hidden horse maintenance costs.

The new motorbuses and the electric trams had greater range than their horse-drawn predecessors and allowed the public transportation system to push out even further from the center; this had a profound effect on the suburbs. In 1904 the managing director of the London Underground Tramways wrote that the new tram routes had created such a demand for new land, that "estates where one

dwelling formerly stood on its own acreage now are being cut up into building plots for houses that average 20 or 30 to the acre."

Drifting into the Great War

The drift to war in Europe in the summer of 1914 had proved unstoppable and when the German army

By 1905 there were several companies operating motorbuses in the city, including the London General Omnibus Company. In 1906 there were only 241 motorbuses on the streets compared with 3,484 horse-drawn omnibuses (which had changed little since the days of Shillibeer's first model from 1829, left); a year later the number of horse-drawn omnibuses had fallen to 2,557, the number of motorbuses had risen to 1,205. Between 1909 and 1911 the L.G.O.C. took over most of its major rivals and restored its position of near-monopoly of bus services in London. By 1912 there were only 376 horse-drawn buses left in London. The rate of technological advance in the first few years of the 20th century was astonishing; in just ten years the motor-bus completely replaced the omnibus. The last horse-drawn omnibus ran between Peckham and Honor Oak in South London on August 4, 1914.

invaded Belgium, Britain declared war. In London the news of war was greeted with mixed feelings. The journalist Michael MacDonagh recorded in his diary that "making my way to Trafalgar Square, I found two rival demonstrations in progress under Nelson's Pillar—on one side of the plinth for war, and on the other against! The rival crowds glared at each

other. Cries of 'The War does not concern us; we must keep out of it!' were answered with cries of 'Down with Germany, the violator of Belgium!' At Buckingham Palace, the king came out onto the balcony and the crowd sang the national anthem."

The initial impact of the war was a decline in some peacetime industries, and in the demand for exports. This caused unemployment; hotel workers, builders, clothing and textile workers were among the worst affected, but many manufacturers suffered. By April 1915 London had recovered and the war economy had created almost full employment. Despite the close historical ties between Britain and Germany, anti-German sentiments began to appear.

In formerly remote and middle-class suburbs, such as Hammersmith, Ealing, Tooting, Lewisham and Norwood the new trams and bus routes were bringing working-class settlers. The tram was cheap, speedy and convenient, as one commentator wrote, "family after family are evacuating the blocks and crowded tenements for little four-roomed cottages, with little gardens, at Hither Green or Tooting."

Most Germans and Austrians had left Britain at the start of the war; those who stayed were interned as enemy aliens. People of German descent changed their names to sound more English; most famously, King George V changed his family name from the very German Saxe-Coburg Gotha to the very English "Windsor."

The first air raids

For the first time in a foreign war Londoners were on the front line; the city was a target for the airplanes and airships of the German army and navy. The first air raids over London were carried out by Zeppelin airships on May 31, 1915, the eighth Zeppelin raid of the War. The Germans reached the outskirts of London. Guns had been placed in a defensive ring around Greater London, but they

were ineffective against the Zeppelins. Although Zeppelins would continue to raid into 1917, their increasing vulnerability to the city's defenses made their raids virtually suicidal. Instead the Germans sent in Gotha bombers, and later the "Giants" to attack London. The massive Giants were the largest hostile aircraft that ever have flown in British air space; their wing span at 138 feet 6 inches, was just three feet shorter than that of the more modern B-29 Superfortress.

The air raids were taking their toll on the spirit of the people. Lloyd George, the Prime Minister, recorded in his memoirs that: "There was grave and

London was slowly put on a war footing; hotels and large houses were commandeered for use as billets, military or government offices or hospitals. Parks and open spaces were converted into allotments to grow food or camps for the troops. To control drinking that might interfere with war production, pubs were forced to close at 10pm and the buying of drinks for other people was prohibited. Regulation of drinking did have some success: in 1914 there were 67,103 incidents of drunkenness in London; by 1917 this had fallen to 16,567. It took until the beginning of the 21st century to restore full drinking hours. Pictured is the lavishly decorated The Salisbury in St. Martin's Lane.

growing panic among the population in the East End where the attack had taken place. At the slightest rumor of approaching airplanes, tubes and tunnels were packed with panic-stricken men, women and children. Every clear night the commons around London were black with refugees from the threatened metropolis."

But, he added, "it is right, however, to record the fact that the undoubted terror did not swell by a single murmur the demand for peace."

In all, nearly 100 tons of bombs were dropped on London causing £2,000,000 worth of damage, 670 people were killed and 1,960 were injured.

America joins the war

On April 6, 1917, the United States entered the war against Germany. In London the news of the American entry brought relief. In the streets Londoners wore U.S. flag pins. The Stars and Stripes was flown in Downing Street and alongside the Union Jack over the houses of Parliament. This was the first time another nation's flag had ever flown above the Parliament buildings. Four months later in August, U.S. soldiers paraded through London for the first time and were cheered by crowds along the street.

With the entry of the United States into the war

In early 1916 London's defenses were remodelled. Additional guns were placed in Regents Park and on Tower Bridge. The defenses were much more effective and on the night of September 24, 1916, Zeppelin L33 was shot down by gunfire over London. But the greatest danger to the hydrogen-filled Zeppelins were airplanes using newly developed incendiary bullets which could set them on fire. By the end of 1916 the Germans had lost eight Zeppelins on raids over Britain, four of them on raids over London.

the defeat of the Germans was inevitable; it came on November 11, 1918, known as Armistice Day. In London there were celebrations in every street. Later a huge fire was started in Trafalgar Square that seriously damaged the base of Nelson's Column (the damage can still be seen today).

But London had paid a high price for the victory. War memorials were erected in every borough or parish and virtually every family had lost one member in the war.

Weakened in the war's aftermath

With the war over, Londoners tried to return to normal. Women left the heavy industrial jobs they had taken during the war, although they remained in many of the various clerical and retail jobs they had taken. Trade and finance had been disrupted, but they slowly recovered during the 1920s. The tonnage of shipping using the Port of London had declined by over 50 percent during the war, but by the 1920s trade was beginning to recover. In the City, financial dealing slowly recovered, London became a center of foreign exchange, and there was a boom in the insurance market.

However, the cost of the war had weakened the British economy and London found it difficult to maintain its dominant position in world finance. The British pound had lost its prestige and gave way to the U.S. dollar. The economic and industrial power of the United States led to that country ultimately taking Britain's role as the world's leading creditor and investor.

But not everything was gloomy and as if to demonstrate this in 1924-25 the Government staged the British Empire Exhibition at Wembley in west London. Elsewhere in London the needs of

Two years after the end of the Great War, on Armistice Day 1920, the king attended the burial of the Unknown Warrior at Westminster Abbey. The coffin was brought through the streets of London on a gun carriage drawn by six black horses. En route the king unveiled the Cenotaph in Whitehall, designed by the architect Sir Edward Lutyens as a memorial to all the British dead of the war. The Unknown Warrior was buried with full honors in the great abbey. The following year he was posthumously awarded the Congressional Medal of Honor by the U.S. government, which hangs by the grave.

The British Empire Exhibition of 1924/25 was designed to be a celebration of the British Empire, and to strengthen the bonds between the mother country and her imperial possessions. In the words of the official guidebook, it was "a family party of the British Empire—the First Family Party since the Great War, when the whole world opened its astonished eyes to see that an Empire with a hundred languages and races had but one soul and mind." Each colony of the Empire was represented by its own pavilion and there were other buildings to show Industry, the Arts and Engineering and even the work of the British Government. The Exhibition attracted 17,500,000 visitors; few of them probably realized that the Exhibition was a symbol of an age past and that in the space of less than a lifetime the Empire would be gone.

commerce and trade were creating new buildings and opportunities. The face of London was being radically altered. Regent Street, Nash's elegant road of the 1820s, was deemed too small for modern retailers and between 1920 and 1926 it was completely rebuilt. New buildings, shops and offices replaced older and often historic buildings. The aristocracy were selling property and moving out of London and their place was taken by large corporations and businesses. The Edwardian Baroque and the Grand Manner was still popular for official and commercial buildings, but new building techniques and ideas from Europe and the United States were introducing Art-Deco styles and Modernism into London's architecture.

City at leisure

The interwar years were the Roaring Twenties and the Jazz Age. Despite the problems of poverty, unemployment and the Great Depression it was an age when those who could enjoy themselves did. Many new nightclubs were started in London where the well-to-do could party, dance and drink champagne until the early hours. Although the singalong Musical Hall entertainment was in decline, cabaret and vaudeville revues were still popular, and in the established theater the accurately-observed and often comic plays of Noel Coward were popular with

middle-class and aristocratic audiences alike. Londoners also could go to the cinema. By 1932 the County of London had 258 cinemas with 344,000 seats, one for every 13 Londoners, and by 1939 virtually every suburb of London had a cinema.

For those who wished to have their entertainment at home the British Broadcasting Corporation was founded in 1922 and made its first radio broadcast from Savoy Hill off the Strand. By 1925 it was possible to hear the London programs all over the Britain. In 1936 the B.B.C. broadcast its first television program from the Alexandra Palace.

The development of television was rapid; the Coronation procession of George VI (1937-1952) was televized in 1937, as was the Wimbledon tennis tournament the following month. Major sporting events were screened in 1938, as was the arrival in 1938 of Prime Minister Neville Chamberlain after his meeting in Munich with Adolph Hitler. With the outbreak of war, television was shut down until 1946.

Not all recreation involved being inside. London's transportation system also allowed many to take vacations in the many coastal resorts within easy reach of the capital. For the wealthy traveler it was possible to fly out of London. In 1920 London's first international airport, with customs facilities, opened at Croydon, where it was possible to get a flight to Paris, Amsterdam, Rotterdam, or Berlin. During the Second World War Croydon Airport was used by the military and at the end of the war it was decided to build a new airport at Heathrow, which opened in 1946. For the poorest Londoners hop-picking in Kent provided a popular vacation. Large numbers of Londoners would descend on the hop fields in the summer, where farmers would provide accommodation and beer in return for labor.

London also had a thriving film industry. The first British talkie was made in 1929 by Alfred Hitchcock (below), produced by British International Pictures in Elsetree (pictured below, left) in north London whose studio was nicknamed the British Hollywood. There were several other successful motion picture-makers around London like

Gainsborough, Gaumont British, Ealing Studios among others. The great director Alexander Korda worked in Elstree and many of the great British stars like Vivien Leigh, Laurence Olivier, Ralph Richardson, John Gielgud and Margaret Lockwood made their movie debuts for London filmmakers in the inter-war period.

Metro-Land

The interwar years saw further growth in the outer
suburbs that formed Metropolitan London while the
population of the County of London fell. Between
1901 and 1911 the population of the County of
London fell by 14,500 whereas the population of
Metropolitan London increased by just under
654,000. This trend continued in the interwar years
with the population of the County of London falling
by half a million between 1911 and 1939 to 4,013,400
while Metropolitan London's population increased by
just under 1.5 million in the same period to 8,615,050.
This movement had begun with the expansion of the
public transportation network as a result of
electrification, and the introduction of the motorbus.
In the interwar years, further developments in public
transportation, the construction of new arterial roads
and the rise in the number of privately-owned
automobiles all increased the trend. By 1939 London
was physically twice as large as it had been in 1914
and six times larger than it was in 1880.

At the same time, the Underground railway
companies were pushing the bounds of suburbia out
from the center of London. The U.E.R.L. had

During the 1920s the
London General
Omnibus Company
(L.G.O.C.) began to
restore its virtual
monopoly in motorbus
routes, after losing its
dominant position
during the war. Larger
buses capable of
carrying up to 60
people were introduced,
new buses were given
more comfortable
accommodation, the
upper deck was roofed
over and the seats were
upholstered. In 1926
pneumatic tires were
fitted for the first time,
and the speed limit was
raised from 12 to 20
m.p.h. The developments
in bus design and
comfort made them a
popular mode of
transport. In 1920, buses
carried 930 million
passengers a year; by
1938 they carried just
over 4,000 million
passengers. Much of this
growth was at the
expense of the less
flexible electric trams. By
1923 most of London's
tram routes were
operating at a loss.
They were replaced
with trolleybuses,
basically electric buses
that ran on tires rather
than rails. The last
London tram was taken
out of service in 1952.
But the trolleybus was
also uneconomical and
taken out of service in
1962.

recovered from its prewar financial crisis, and during the 1920s and 1930s, rapidly expanded its network. The Northern Line was extended to Morden and Edgware in 1922-24, and the Piccadilly Line was pushed out to Cockfosters and Hounslow between 1932 and 1933. The independent Metropolitan Railway even had its own house-building company to produce Garden Estates along its lines. In its advertising, the Railway called it "Metro-Land," a name that has stuck ever since and has become an all-embracing term for suburbia. The Metropolitan Railway constructed ten housing estates and 13 golf courses along its line at Wembley Park, Neasden, Rickmansworth and Pinner. By 1939 the company had built 4,600 houses.

Traffic pumps through the arteries

During the 1920s, as part of a scheme to reduce congestion on the main routes in and out of London, as well as a means of creating employment, the government set out on several road-building schemes. The results were several new main routes out of London, the Great West Road, (to the west), the Great Cambridge Road (to the north), Eastern Avenue (to the east) and Western Avenue built to replace the old London-to-Oxford road. There were new bypasses built around suburban town centers. The North Circular Road was constructed to link the new arterial routes and provide an east–west route around north London; a South Circular Road was planned for south London but was never completed. The new arterial roads encouraged ribbon development of houses, shops and factories. The Great West Road attracted splendid Art-Deco style factories, the best examples were erected by Firestone (now sadly demolished) and Hoover.

The trend for London to spill out into adjacent counties caused some concern. The

All the existing buses, trains and trams were united in 1933 under the London Passenger Transport Board, known as London Transport (L.T.). Architects were brought in to design the new stations, which today are regarded as superb examples of modern architectural design, such as Arnos Grove (pictured below). After the war, L.T. was taken into national ownership but has now been controversially sold into privatization. Londoners still pay more for using their metro system than the inhabitants of any other city in the world. Two million passengers use the Tube daily, but humans are not the only inhabitants —it is also home to an estimated half-a-million mice and rats, including a species that has become resistant to most poisons. There is a type of mosquito in the deepest tunnels that has been there so long it has evolved into an entirely new sub-species. There are also pigeons that regularly hitch rides in Tube trains.

positioning of stations and the routes of the new arterial roads rather than any grand design controlled suburban growth. Even the L.C.C.'s program of slum clearance and rehousing had contributed to the problem by creating new housing estates beyond the L.C.C. boundary. The idea of constructing a Green Belt of protected undeveloped countryside around London had been proposed as early as 1890. Following the Town and Country Planning Act of 1932 the L.C.C. began to work on a London-wide development plan, and in 1935 they began a policy of subsidizing those local authorities that wished to purchase and preserve undeveloped land. By 1938 the L.C.C. had secured 13,000 acres for the Green Belt and was in the process of adding a further 60,000 acres to the scheme. The authority proudly stated that it had a "remarkable variety of natural country—farmland, pastureland, woodland, heather, downland, stretches of water, riversides and natural skylines—and in some cases land for playing fields," and that the land was "not only preserved for all time from building, but is held on conditions which provide for the greatest amount of public access."

The inter-war years saw an explosion of new construction, most evident in the stylish factories within the city. Camden Town's Art-Deco Carreras cigarette factory, built between 1926 and 1928, was the world's largest wholly reinforced concrete building at the time. The Egyptian façade celebrated the recent discovery of Tutankhamun's tomb.

Slums and strikes

Despite the development of the suburbs and the creation by the L.C.C. of new inner-city housing and suburban garden estates, there still remained vast areas of inner London where slum conditions and

vo Hundred Jarrow Men Step Out
ravely on Their Trek to London
rrving Town's Hopes With Them

HOP'S BLESSING
R CRUSADE TO
D UNEMPLOYMENT

Although London was spared the worst of the Depression, the 1930s were still years of high unemployment and industrial unrest. On October 18 1932, some 2,000 unemployed workers clashed with police at St. George's Circus and outside County Hall in South London during the march led by the Communist National Unemployed Workers Movement (N.U.W.M.). By the time the march reached Hyde Park it was estimated to be 100,000 strong. There were more scuffles with the police. Three days later an even larger crowd gathered in Trafalgar Square and again there was fighting with the police. The marchers continued to protest until November 5 when they began to disperse. There were 45 arrests including the Communist leadership of the N.U.W.M. But another N.U.W.M.-organized march went off peacefully in 1934 and when the huge numbers of unemployed Jarrow marchers arrived in London from the North in 1936 there was no violence.

poverty were common. It has been estimated that as many as 21 percent of London households lived in poverty in 1929. One survey found that the highest cause of poverty (48 percent) was as a result of unemployment.

The economic problems of the 1920s and 1930s saw considerable periods of unrest and unemployment in London. Between 1921 and 1936 there were 181 large strikes in London. There was a general fear that economic hardship, military demobilization and the ideology of Soviet Russia might spread revolution and anarchy in Britain. As the head of the Metropolitan Police told the Cabinet "in the event of rioting, for the first time in history the rioters will be better trained than the troops." Even the Metropolitan Police had gone on strike for a week in 1918, raising fear that they might be unreliable in an emergency.

There were frequent marches and protests by unemployed workers during 1920 and 1921, and these often ended in violence and riot when the police broke them up. In 1926 the Trades Union Congress called a general strike in support of striking miners. In London the response among industrial workers was immediate, and the government was forced to call on volunteers and the military to keep London's transport systems and power stations running. The strike ran for six days before it was called off. In that time there had been battles between strikers and police in New Cross, Deptford and Poplar and stones had been thrown at buses driven by strike-breakers.

The Blitz

On September 3, 1939 Great Britain had declared war on Germany after that country refused to withdraw its forces from Poland. The experience of the First World War had made the authorities fearful of the casualties and damage that an air offensive against London might cause, and as the European situation had deteriorated and war seemed more likely in the late 1930s, preparations had already begun in London.

Some Londoners took the opportunity to move out of inner London, altogether to the safer suburbs; others just left for the night. At the height of the Blitz about 5,000 East Enders camped out in Epping Forest, while in the southeastern suburbs of Kent about 15,000 people slept in the Chiselhurst Caves. Although Underground stations had been used as shelters during the First World War, the Government was determined to prevent this from happening again and banned their use as shelters during air raids. But when a huge crowd assembled outside Liverpool Street Underground station demanding to take shelter, the authorities gave way and accepted the use of the Underground as a shelter.

Beds were brought in and even entertainment was arranged. Fifteen miles of platforms and tunnels were brought into use and on one night in September 1940, 177,000 people were recorded as taking shelter in the Underground. By February 1941 there was sufficient air-raid shelter accommodation for 92 percent of London's population, although it was calculated that 60 percent of Londoners sought no protection at all. The Underground and other shelters sometimes offered a false sense of security. The Anderson shelters, built in the backyards of homes,

Against the backdrop of industrial unrest, unemployment and Communist agitation, Sir Oswald Mosley formed the British Union of Fascists (B.U.F.) known as the "Blackshirts." Between 1934 and 1935 the B.U.F. gained a reputation for brutality and violence as well as anti-Semitic views. In 1936 a march by 3,000 Blackshirts through Stepney was rerouted by police when 100,000 anti-Fascist demonstrators barred their way. The street fight has since become famous as the "Battle of Cable Street" (painted above in a mural in the street). Despite their meetings and rallies, neither the Communists nor the Fascists ever enjoyed widespread support in London, where voters' allegiance to the mainstream parties was always too strong for them to break.

Aside from the terrible loss of life to Londoners, the Blitz's destruction on the ground was indiscriminate. Pictured is one example of the damage, the ruins of Temple Church in the City of London, which were destroyed after the raid of May 10, 1941. Between 1936 and the first German air attacks of 1940, the London Boroughs and the L.C.C. prepared fire precaution schemes and began to stockpile fire-fighting equipment. Auxiliary firefighters were recruited. Work also began on the construction of new emergency water supplies. There was a fear that the Germans would use poison gas so in 1938 every Londoner was issued a gas mask. Air Raid Wardens Organizations were set up as a civil defense force in the event of air attack, and Boroughs began to run training courses for volunteer wardens. On the outbreak of the war, formal Air Raid Precautions (A.R.P.) posts were established in case of air attack. Learning the lessons of the First World War, women (under the age of 50) found themselves eligible to be conscripted for war work.

were the standard shelters issued by the Government but they only offered limited protection: tests had shown that it was were effective against a 500-pound bomb exploding 40 feet away. Other shelters such as steel-framed buildings and railway arches were as vulnerable to bombs as any other buildings. In 1944 a

direct hit by a V1 flying bomb on Lewisham High Street demolished a subterranean public shelter, a bus and several shops. Fifty-one people died (to this day they are not all identified), 124 people were badly injured and 187 suffered lesser injuries.

Even when Londoners took refuge in the deep-level Underground system they were not always safe. Seven people were killed by a bomb at Trafalgar Square Station, another 20 died when Marble Arch Station was hit and 19 were killed at Bounds Green. The worst incident at Underground stations was the death of 64 people at Balham, when a bomb caused the road above the tunnel to collapse and a mixture of rubble and public-supply water to flood down into the station below. At Bank, 117 people died when the station received a direct hit, and at Bethnal Green Station 178 people were crushed or suffocated on the stairs during a rush to get into the shelter one night in March 1943.

In the last few days of peace London made its final preparations for war. Buildings were sandbagged to provide protection from bomb blasts, and a blackout was introduced. Trenches were dug across parks and open spaces to prevent aircraft from landing and road signs and station name boards were

By the end of 1938 some public air raid shelters had already been constructed and the decision had been made to issue each household a corrugated steel "Anderson shelter" (pictured left). These could accommodate four to five people and were to be constructed either inside a house or half-buried in the garden, and covered with earth. Inside, it was cramped, damp and with few creature comforts. By April 1940, more than 2,000,000 had been issued. One Londoner remembered using these shelters in 1940 and 1941: "We used to go in the shelter when the Battle of Britain was on, but when the Blitz came we used to live down there. You'd hear the sirens go off at 6 or 7 o'clock at night, and you would collect up your belongings. And you would live there for the rest of the night until the sirens went in the morning." Public shelters were also provided by the authorities. Trenches were dug in London's parks and communal shelters were created in basements, large steel-framed buildings, basements and railway arches. There were also some purpose-built brick shelters above ground.

While adult Londoners immediately joined the war effort in and around the city—such as these workers buying newspapers as they leave a war factory near the capital —prewar plans to evacuate children and mothers out of London were put into action following the German invasion of Poland in 1939. Within three days, 393,700 children, 50,000 teachers and 257,000 mothers and young children were moved out of the metropolis. Evacuation proved to be unpopular both with the children and the parents left behind. By Christmas 1939 about 34 percent of evacuated children and 90 percent of mothers and babies had returned to London. When the government, led by Winston Churchill (pictured below), tried to re-establish evacuation in mid-1940 the response was small and by this time more children were returning than were leaving.

removed. In expectation of the bombardment of the city, hospitals were made ready for casualties, ambulances were assembled and additional mortuaries were set up equipped with a supply of papier-maché coffins.

The defense of London

The defense of London was also taken in hand. Fighter squadrons were prepared, and barrage balloons were flown above the city. Searchlights and anti-aircraft (ack-ack) guns were positioned anywhere that space could be found. Their crews were treated like heroes and were welcomed into local homes.

The initial months of the war were uneventful and known as the "Phoney War," and there was little impact on the lives of Londoners. But in May 1940 the German offensive began in strength, and by the end of June the Nazis had overrun Norway, France and the Low Countries. The British Army was pushed back to the French port town of Dunkirk and in the so-called Miracle of Dunkirk 340,000 British and French troops were rescued from the from beach. Prime minister Winston Churchill (1874-1965) told the nation "the Battle of France is over, the Battle of Britain is about to begin." The Germans believed that their air force, the Luftwaffe, had to gain air

"LET US GO FORWARD TOGETHER"

St. Paul's Cathedral was hit by 28 incendiary bombs durng the devastating raid of December 27-28. It was only the dedication of the fire watchers on the great church's roof that saved the building. The survival of St. Paul's became a powerful symbol to the Londoners of their resolve "to see it through." This is a view of the intact cathedral seen from the wreckage in nearby Queen Victoria Street.

superiority to ensure the success of their Invasion of
England (Operation Sea Lion). But the Germans did
not attack immediately after their conquest of France;
instead, there was a few weeks' delay, enough to allow
Britain's Royal Air Force (R.A.F.) to make some
preparations for the battle. The Battle of Britain

The Battle of Britain
took place when the
Luftwaffe attempted to
win air superiority over
southern England from
the Royal Air Force as
an essential prerequisite
for the invasion of Great

began on July 10, 1940 with
an attack by German aircraft
on shipping in the Channel
and the Channel Ports. The
Germans had a force of 2,600
bombers; the total strength of
the R.A.F. fighter command
was 640.

London soon became the
main target. At five o'clock in
the afternoon on September 7
1940 a flight of 320 German
bombers escorted by 600
fighters attacked London.

This was the start of 76 consecutive nights (with just
one exception) of bombing and was the first day of
the Battle of London. The R.A.F. slowly started to
build up strength and to gain the upper hand. The
Battle of London continued into the spring of 1941,
but the raids were becoming more and more sporadic.
But the Germans were still capable of launching
major attacks. The deaths and damage continued to
mount as the bombs and fires took their grim toll. By
the time the Blitz was over, London had been
subjected to 19,000 tons of high explosive but had
survived. It had not collapsed into panic and madness
as had been predicted in the 1930s, but 375,000
Londoners were left homeless, and more than 15,000
had lost their lives.

Britain by German naval
and land forces. The
Spitfire fighter (seen
here at the Imperial War
Museum) was key in
pushing back the waves
of the infinitely more
numerous Luftwaffe
planes.

The list of buildings destroyed or damaged in one
of the raids reads like a "who's who" of London and
England's heritage: the Chamber of the House of
Commons was destroyed and several churches, St.
James's Palace, Lambeth Palace and Westminster

"NEVER WAS SO MUCH
OWED BY SO MANY
TO SO FEW"

Abbey, Westminster Hall, the House of Lords, the Tower of London and the Mansion House, to name a few, were all damaged.

The G.I.s arrive

In 1940 and for much of 1941, Britain, and London in particular faced Germany alone, but on December 7, 1941 the Japanese launched their surprise attack on the United States Navy at Pearl Harbor and the United States entered the Second World War. Within months the first G.I.s were arriving in London. Throughout the war London had become home to a whole variety of soldiers of different nationalities: there were Canadians, Free French, Czech, Poles and Dutch as well as soldiers from every nation in Europe occupied by the Nazis.

The presence of so many G.I.s provoked mixed feelings among Londoners. The Americans were better paid, better nourished and more confident than the British soldiers who had been through two years of war, defeat and deprivation. This was a constant cause of resentment as was the popularity of the G.I.s with the women of London. But the feelings of antagonism were not universal. Most Londoners liked their U.S. allies, seeing them as kind, friendly and generous. They were a welcome relief from the monotony of the war and a colorful symbol that Britain was no longer alone. For the G.I.s too London was not always unwelcoming; one 19-year-old serviceman from Oklahoma wrote: "The conviviality of London in wartime was unimaginable: everyone was real friendly."

Doodlebugs and the Baby Blitz

In the years following the Blitz London's defenses were improved and although there were occasional raids there was no attempt to sustain an air offensive until the Germans launched the "Baby Blitz "on January 21, 1944. The raids were launched between nine o'clock in the evening and half past four in the

The West End particularly was colonized by U.S. servicemen. The first to arrive had been given accommodation in

Piccadilly, and it was said that by the end of 1942 they had completely taken over Grosvenor Square. There was an explosion of U.S. clubs and pubs: the Washington Hotel in Carson Street became the American Red Cross Club, and at the corner of Piccadilly Circus and Shaftsbury Avenue was Rainbow Corner, a club where two huge dining rooms, seating 2,000 people, provided American food 24 hours a day.
Overleaf: Piccadilly Circus and its surrounding bars, clubs and theaters was a popular focus for entertainment during the war.

morning and consisted of some 450 bombing sorties when about 2,000 tons of explosives and incendiary bombs were dropped. This was to be the last of the Luftwaffe's bombing campaigns over London and much of their earlier firepower had gone. Indeed, following the first raid the impact of the bombing decreased and mid-April saw the last German air raid over London.

That same year Hitler launched his two secret vengeance weapons against London, the V1 Flying bomb (called "buzz bombs" or "doodlebugs" by Londoners because of the noise they made in the air) and the V2 rocket. The first V1s hit London in June 1944. Unmanned rocket powered missiles they were launched from occupied Europe in the direction of London and fell to the ground when they ran out of fuel. The damage they caused was slight compared to the air raids London had already suffered but they were so random that they strained the morale of most Londoners. V1s continued to bomb London until March 1945, by which time they had killed 5,000 people and injured 15,000 others.

Counting the cost of victory

On May 8, 1945 Germany surrendered, followed by Japan in the Far East on August 6. Londoners turned out in their thousands to celebrate in Trafalgar Square. The crowds surged in front of Buckingham Palace and called for the King. Others had been at Westminster to cheer Churchill.

But London and her citizens had paid a high price for their victory. London had suffered 354 air raids by piloted craft and 2,937 by pilotless rockets and

On the night of December 27/28 London suffered one of the most devastating raids of the war. That night 136 Luftwaffe bombers concentrated their attack on the City itself. The City was deserted, and the fire-watching precautions taken were insufficient. The Luftwaffe bombs started 1,400 fires in a small area of the city centered around St Paul's. There was an acute shortage of water; the City's water mains were broken and the Thames was particularly low. Most of the fires burned out of control. One of them covered an area of half a square mile — 163 people died including 16 fire fighters. The raid devastated the historic heart of the City — the Guildhall was burnt to a shell and eight of Wren's churches were gutted, along with All Hallows by the Tower, several Livery Company Halls, the Wood Street Telephone Exchange and the Central Telegraph Office. Nine hospitals, five main line railway terminals, and sixteen Underground stations were all damaged. Later the Nazis turned to raids on London using the V1 (known as "doodle-bugs") and V2 flying bombs launched from across the English Channel.

missiles. Some 29,890 Londoners were dead and a further 50,000 were badly injured. The national total for the whole war was 60,595 and 86,182 respectively. A total of 116,000 houses, including 50,000 in the L.C.C. area, had been destroyed, 288,000 needed major repairs and a further 1,000,000 needed repairs of some sort.

Industry decreased as companies took the opportunities of bomb-damage insurance to relocate. There had been rationing and shortages, and basic foods continued to be rationed even after the war had ended. Things were never quite the same again. The United States and Soviet Russia were now the unquestioned dominant world superpowers, as Britain and France's humiliation over the Suez Crisis (when Egypt snatched control of the Suez Canal from them) in 1956 clearly illustrated. The beginning of the end for the British Empire was marked in August 1947 when India—"the Jewel in the Crown"—gained her independence. London's role as an imperial capital was waning. Nevertheless things did seem to be going well; the landslide election of a Labour Government in 1946 ushered in

Of the 460 acres of buildings in the City, 164 had been laid waste by the War's end. The Guildhall was a burned-out shell, 18 city churches, 14 by Wren, lay in ruins. The Inns of Court had all been damaged, and the British Museum was badly hit with the loss of 150,000 books from the British Library. At the museum's branch in Colindale, 30,000 volumes of newspapers were lost. In the suburbs, Southwark and Bermondsey lost 15 percent of their built-up area; the other boroughs lost between 5 and 10 percent. It is still possible to see areas of undeveloped bomb-damaged land in parts of London even today.

the Welfare State and there was a general feeling of wellbeing, prosperity and security in the nation.

London rebuilds

Despite all the damage London set about rebuilding just as she had done after the Great Fire of 1666. Shops and businesses were rebuilt, and by 1954 central London had as much office space as it had had before the war. In the City many of the bombed-out industries left for the suburbs and the new towns, and the Square Mile became even more dominated by the needs of banking and finance. Height restrictions introduced in 1894 were abolished and Upper and Lower Thames Street were widened to form a main east–west route through the City, finally cutting the City off from the Thames.

The architecture of the rebuilding of London was a mix of traditional styles and modernism. The use of traditional architectural styles provoked criticism among progressive architects and was described as "a style of timidity, of playing safe, of introducing just enough of the 20th century to avoid being ridiculous and keeping just enough of giant columns and other paraphenalia of Empire to stake a claim of remaining a great nation."

Ultimately, the dominant style was a British interpretation of the business architecture of the United States where there was an "assimilation of Modernism into the commercial mainstream."

Move to the Green Belt

The biggest task facing the London Boroughs and the L.C.C.

One of the most visible results of the rebuilding in the City was the Barbican development on 16 acres of bomb-damaged land to the north of St. Paul's. The complex included a library, school, exhibition and concert hall and the Museum of London. Accommodation was provided by a mix of low and high-rise buildings—the latter were the highest in Europe when they were first built.

was rehousing those whose homes had been bombed. In 1943, J. H. Forshaw, the L.C.C.'s architect, and Patrick Abercrombie, professor of town planning at University College, London, produced the "County of London Plan," followed in 1944 by Abrecrombie's "Greater London Plan," where he anticipated the development of London up to 30 miles out from the City. In

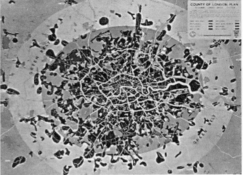

1947, legislation was passed to put the two plans into effect. Some of the schemes were never fully implemented—it was never possible to double the amount of open space in inner London, and many of the suggested roads were never built. Nevertheless, these two documents formed the basis for London's urban planning for 30 years after the war.

Abercrombie had advocated the preservation of the "Green Belt" scheme begun by the L.C.C.. This was confirmed and enlarged by Parliament; between 1956 and 1961 the Green Belt was extended from 800 to 2000 square miles, with even further additions in the 1980s. The reports had also suggested the construction of satellite "new towns" between 20 and 30 miles out from the center of London, and in 1947-48 the "New Towns" of Basildon, Bracknell, Crawley, Harlow, Hatfield, Hemel Hempstead, Stevenage, and Welwyn Garden City were built. The new towns proved very successful, and since their establishment their populations have soared far above the 60,000 people they were intended to hold.

The new homes scheme in the postwar 1940s envisaged that the new towns would be medium-sized and self-contained communities of up to 60,000 people living in good affordable council housing. The towns were to have their own infrastructure free of London, they would have shopping centers, schools, churches and industry, which would be relocated from Central London. Each new town would be surrounded by green countryside—the Green Belt—intended to contain the outward expansion of the capital. However, it is the freeing-up of London's Green Belt that has turned out to be a source of constant controversy as private developers, local councils and the national government have pressed to build in it, mostly citing the pressing need for new homes.

"10,000 dwellings a year"

In the inner city the devastation caused by the bombing allowed, for the first time, mass rebuilding. The great slum areas that had plagued London for 200 years, and had defied any attempts to improve and redevelop them, were in many cases rebuilt. The Lansbury Estate in Poplar was rebuilt as part of the Festival of Britain's Exhibition of Living Architecture and was supposed to act as a blueprint for the redevelopment of deprived,

inner city areas. It was a mix of low and high-rise accommodation, with schools, shops, churches and plenty of open space. Unfortunately the adventurous scheme failed, as it was expensive and did not translate well to mass production. By 1949 the L.C.C. had built 50,000 new dwellings, mainly in blocks of between 4-6 stories high. Between 1948 and 1963 the L.C.C. and the London Boroughs built housing at the rate of 10,000 dwellings a year.

The Festival of Britain

Rebuilding the city and the growth of the welfare state encouraged faith in the future of London. In 1948 the capital hosted the Olympics, and in 1951, as a symbol of the end of postwar austerity, the Government held the Festival of Britain Exhibition.

The exhibition was based on the Great Exhibition of 1851 and although there were events throughout the country the main exhibitions were centered on 27 acres of derelict land on the South Bank of the Thames. With the same spirit as the British Empire

Inspired by the boom in post-war modern buildings in central London, the outer boroughs turned to the construction of high-rise apartments. Dubbed "tower blocks," these were significantly more expensive to build than low-rise estates, but the Government and town planners had great faith in them. They promised to provide high-density family accommodation in the confined spaces available in the inner cities. Tower blocks such as Trellis Tower (pictured) were seen as architectural splendors that would grace the skyline and create communities in the sky. As a result they attracted government support and subsidies between 1956 and 1968. It was understood that no more than 40 percent of Londoners would want to live in tower blocks and they only ever formed a quarter of the public housing stock built between 1945 and 1975. The building of tower blocks stopped when the subsidy for their construction was ended. Furthermore, they never lived up to the dreams of the town planners and, rightly or wrongly, have become a symbol of inner-city decay and all that was wrong with postwar urban planning.

Exhibition of 1924, this was a patriotic and morale-boosting exercise to show both the population and the world that Britain was still great. Eight million people visited the festival and the poet Dylan Thomas described it as "a palace in thunderland, sizzling with scientific witches' brews." But it was to be the last of the Great Exhibitions, and when the Government tried to resurrect the idea for the Millennium Dome in Greenwich for the year 2000, the concept proved a humiliating failure.

A new Elizabethan Age

In 1953 King George VI died. He was succeeded by his young daughter Elizabeth II. The coronation in Westminster Abbey was a spectacular of pomp and ceremony that was televized by the B.B.C. in a ground-breaking broadcast. The coronation drew the nation, Empire and Commonwealth together and held out the promise of a new Elizabethan Age. In 1959, the prime minister Harold Macmillan was able to say with some justification that "many of our people have never had it so good." London was also becoming cleaner. Since the 19th century and before, the city had been plagued with fogs that Londoners cheerfully called "pea-soupers." But the fogs had a sinister side too; the Great Smog of 1952 had 4,000 premature deaths attributed to it. Clean Air Acts followed and the decline in domestic fires and industrial smoke pollution meant that the Great Smog was the last.

But the times were changing. In 1965 the L.C.C. was abolished and replaced by the Greater London Council (G.L.C.). The G.L.C. had authority over the entire Metropolitan London area, a space four times as large as the old L.C.C. jurisdiction. The G.L.C. was given responsibility

1951's Festival of Britain exhibition on the banks of the Thames was a much-needed morale-booster for the war-torn population of Britain. It was centered on the Dome of Discovery, shown below under construction in 1950. The Dome was four times the size of the Albert Hall, and the Skylon, a huge luminous obelisk-like sculpture of steel and aluminium. There were themed pavilions on subjects like the sea and ships, homes and gardens, and also power and production. The Royal Festival Hall was built as part of the festival and was, intentionally, the only building of the complex to survive demolition. It is now the centerpiece of the South Bank Centre—a vibrant arts complex which also includes the National Theatre, Hayward Gallery and National Film Theatre.

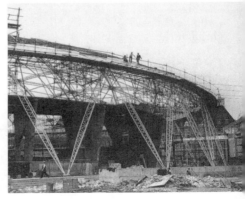

for maintaining the strategic planning for the entire city. Once again the City retained its independence. Among the G.L.C.'s achievements were the building of a new Underground line, the Jubilee Line, in 1978 and the construction of the Thames Barrier at Woolwich to prevent flooding from the Thames in 1972-82. The G.L.C. also attempted to encourage the use of public transportation by dramatically lowering the fares, as was done with the penny fare for the omnibuses of the 19th century. But in 1986, the Conservative government of Margaret Thatcher abolished the G.L.C. This was the result of a bitter political struggle with the London authority, whose offices were strategically sited on the South Bank of the Thames directly opposite the Houses of Parliament. London now found itself as the world's only capital without a mayor or central controlling authority.

But by the late 1990s, it was clear that this had to change. As the government developed a more responsible outlook, a directly elected London-wide authority with an elected mayor on the New York model was advocated. Responding positively to this pressure, in 2000 elections were held for the Greater London Authority (G.L.A.). Heading the new organ-ization is the office of mayor to provide a strategic citywide government. In a ironic link with the past, the first elected mayor was Ken Livingstone, who had been head of the G.L.C. at the time of its abolition by the Conser-vatives. Politics still threatened to sour things when Living-stone was

London's relentless drive to build continues on the Thames as well as on its banks. Near the old Execution Dock, where, at low water, the hanging of pirates was carried out, the bodies being left until three tides had washed over them, stand the huge 65ft-high "piers" of the Thames Barrier. Each pier houses an electro-hydraulic engine to turn the gates of the titanic barrier and each gate has a 3,700-ton counter-balance, intended to stop exceptionally high tides from rushing in to the city upstream and flooding it. Yet even this mighty barrier is a stop-gap measure. Britain continues to tilt towards the south-east at a rate of one foot every 100 years and the polar ice caps continue to melt. The tides, therefore, continue to rise: presently at about the rate of two feet every century.

forced to stand as an independent candidate after he failed to get the endorsement of his party, the ruling Labour Party, who put up an alternative candidate.

Loss of Empire

In the years following the Second World War, London lost her role

as an imperial capital and there seemed little to take its place. The postwar population was declining as more and more people moved out of London to the new towns and beyond. In 1939, the population of Greater London was 8,615,050; by 1951 this had fallen to 8,193,921; and in 1991, the population was 6,554,886. Industry, too, in London was in decline. The amount of trade coming from overseas declined as Imperial territories gained independence. Combined with antiquated working practices and old facilities, this led to a terminal decline in London's seaborne trade and between 1967 and 1981 the docks closed. The closure of the docks put 25,000 people out of work and created domino effects in transport, warehousing and food industries. Other areas were also in decline. Printing and the newspapers moved out of Fleet Street to Canary Wharf, and manufacturing decreased as even prosperous firms relocated out of the city. Some of this decline was offset by the rise in tourism, which generates a large income for the city and by the growth of London's service and financial industries.

The City remains a financial powerhouse, although it is now a player in a world rather than an internal and imperial market. In 1981 the London Docklands Development Corporation was formed to redevelop the abandoned docks in east London. Work began in 1988 (and still continues) on the new development based around Canary Wharf, which is linked to the City by its own light railway system and a modern Underground link, and is the home for London's City Airport. The Wharf is rapidly becoming one of the

London's Mayor sets the annual budget for five organisations. These organizations, which have become known as the "G.L.A. Group," comprise: the Greater London Authority; Transport for London, which provides buses, river services and some light rail services, maintains London's main roads and regulates London's licensed taxi service (and will also run the subway, when it is handed over by central government); the Metropolitan Police Authority, which is responsible for maintaining an effective and efficient police service for London; the London Development Agency, which works with business to sustain and improve London's role as a business center, while increasing economic opportunity for all Londoners; London Fire Brigade, which responds to fires and promotes fire prevention, under the oversight of London Fire and Emergency Planning Authority.

largest business centers in Europe, rivaling even the City, and has attracted banks, newspapers, and financial and insurance businesses. Thanks to its sweeping towers and waterways, it is even becoming a tourist attraction.

Investing in its people

The demographic make-up of London has changed as well with the arrival of large numbers of immigrants from former imperial territories and colonies. A true world capital, London has always owed much of its growth, prosperity and culture to immigrants, but the new arrivals in the 20th century came in numbers that made an instant impact on the face of the metropolis. They came for different reasons and in different waves over the decades of the century. Some came as a result of the two World Wars, some arrived as the British Empire crumbled, some were invited to fill badly-needed jobs, while others have come seeking asylum as a result of continuing conflicts elsewhere in the world.

Street life in London grows ever more exotic with markets like Electric Avenue in Brixton (above), and the spectacular Caribbean-inspired Notting Hill Carnival, now one of the largest street parties in the world. It takes place over the August Bank Holiday weekend and attracts millions of revelers.

An ever-growing number of citizens of the various European Union nations now live and work in London, attracted by the huge range of employment opportunities. Meanwhile, substantial West Indian populations moved to the inner suburbs of Brent, Hackney, Haringey, Notting Hill, Lewisham, Southwark and Lambeth. Hong Kong immigrants settled in Soho and established London's Chinatown, Cypriots went to Finsbury—it has even been said that there are more Cypriots living in North London than in Cyprus. Africans, particularly from West Africa, moved to Newham, Waltham Forest, Merton, and Greenwich. Immigrants arrived from the Indian Subcontinent too: Bangladeshis congregated around

Brick Lane and Spitalfields in the East End, Sikhs and Hindus settled in Southall around Heathrow, while Pakistanis and other Indians moved to Newham, Waltham Forest, Merton, and Greenwich.

Other groups in more recent years have arrived as a result of wars in their own countries, such as Vietnamese, Somalis, Yugoslavians and Afghans. At the higher end of the financial spectrum, significant numbers of Iranians, Arabs, Japanese and Russians, one after another, have colonized parts of surburban London, drawn by its financial services as well as the leisure and shopping on offer. The arrival of so many immigrants created racial tension and the rise of right-wing politics. In the 1960s through to the 1990s there were race riots in some inner city areas.

Nevertheless, the newcomers have also added to the cosmopolitan feeling of the capital, bringing new customs, ideas and foods with them. The spectacular Notting Hill Carnival and the concentration of Indian restaurants in Brick Lane are notable examples. As Ford Maddox Ford wrote: "London is a world town, not because of its vastness; it is vast because of its assimilative powers, because it destroys all race characteristics. A Polish Jew changes into an English Hebrew and then into a Londoner without knowing anything about it. A Berlin Junker turns after a year or two into a presentable Londoner."

Those words were written in 1905, but remain true today as second- and third-generation immigrants see themselves as Londoners first and foremost. And so, albeit in a different way, they are part of a tradition that has continued since the Romans first came to the banks of the Thames some 2,000 years ago.

In true London style, the government proposed a Great Exhibition and Festival for the year 2000 in the spirit of those of 1851, 1924 and 1951. It was planned to have exhibitions on faith, science, technology and so on, all housed in a revolutionary building. The Millennium Dome was the last great building project of 20th-century London. It cost over £750,000,000 pounds to build. It was controversial from the beginning and the exhibition was a failure. Unlike previous decades, Londoners did not need reassurance at the dawn of a new century from what many now consider a symbol of increasing Labour and Conservative corruption in government. Instead, they preferred leisure such as that offered by the London Eye (see overleaf).

CHAPTER 10

A EUROPEAN CITY
LONDON IN THE 21ST CENTURY

Leisure characterizes London of the 21st century. Right is the Palace Theatre, a landmark for being home to producer Cameron Macintosh's long-running musical *Les Miserables*. Above is the London Eye, designed by architect team David Marks and Julia Barfield to celebrate the Millennium and put up by a private consortium. A 300ft-high ferris wheel on the South Bank of the Thames opposite the Houses of Parliament, it takes as many as 25 people per gondola to view the capital from the air.

Londoners at the turn of the Millennium are confident in the prosperity and vitality of their city. The past century had thrown all manner of trials in their way, but London and its inhabitants resiliantly survived the Great Depression, two World Wars and the Blitz—suffering more than 100,000 dead and wounded between 1940 and 1945. Together they had survived the trauma and loss of Empire and the inevitable industrial decline that followed.

The final decades of the 20th century saw a sudden resurgence of entrepreneurism that put London back on the global financial map. The boom harked directly back to the late 18th century when the stock markets, coffeshops and markets swelled with the benefits of the fortunes being made by Londoners across the world. There was also much hardship as little of this money flowed into general society. The city suffered too from the crisis caused by the weakening of its local government by the national government in Westminster.

But the advent of the 21st century saw much of this inequality righted. Significantly, there is now an elected mayor, who heads the Greater London Authority, and between them they coordinate centralized policies—mostly beneficial and often controversial—the like of which have never been seen in London's long history. As Queen Elizabeth II passed the fiftieth year of her reign, the City

At 800ft, the tower at Canary Wharf is one of the tallest in Europe, and spearheads one of the great regeneration schemes in London's history: Docklands. Like the phoenix, this was an area where all industry had died with London's waning as a port, but now it has been reinvented as a world center, this time for business. Millions of square feet of office and retail space have already been constructed since the 1990s with millions more planned. The first tenants moved into Canary Wharf in August 1991. Now, about 95 percent of the existing space is leased with 55,000 people working here.

continues to make laws guaranteeing its independence, and the people regularly take to the streets in protest, Londoners would like to think that their predecessors would not only recognize their city but approve.

And so, London remains a vibrant dynamic metropolis looking toward Europe and the world, secure in its place in the modern world and its place in history. London marches on.

London's democratic heart continues to beat strongly, in events like the Countryside Alliance protest of September 2002 (above), which put 450,000 onto the capital's streets, and more than 1,000,000 protesting against war in Iraq in February 2003.

. . . History in the streets

CHRONOLOGY

B.C.
55   Julius Caesar's first invasion of Britain.

A.D.
43   The Romans invade Britain.

c. 50 The Roman town of Londinium is founded.

61   The Iceni tribe under the leadership of their Queen Boudicca rebel against Roman rule. London is attacked and destroyed and has to be rebuilt after the defeat of the rebellion.

c. 85-90 First London Bridge built.

10-450 Anglo-Saxon settlement of Britain begins. London is abandoned by the Romans.

604   Saeberht, king of the East Saxons, allows a church dedicated to St. Paul to be built in London.

c. 670-680 First written records of the Anglo-Saxon trading settlement of Lundenwic or London.

871   Vikings occupy London.

886   Alfred captures London from the Vikings and become the first King of England. He orders the defenses of London to be rebuilt.

1053 Edward "the Confessor" builds a new palace and abbey at Westminster.

1065 Westminster Abbey consecrated.

1066 Harold II, king of England defeated by the Normans at the Battle of Hastings. London surrenders. William the Conqueror crowned king on Christmas Day.

1077-1078 Work begins on the Tower of London.

1086 Rebuilding of St. Paul's Cathedral begins after the Saxon Cathedral is destroyed by fire.

1097 King William II builds the great hall at Westminster.

1128 First mention of a Guildhall in London.

1162 Knights Templar build their first church in London.

1176 London Bridge rebuilt in stone.

1180 First record of the London Guilds.

1191 Henry FitzAilwin becomes London's first Lord Mayor.

1199 Exchequer established in Westminster.

1215 Magna Carta ensures Courts of Justice stay in Westminster. Charter gives London the right to annually elect a mayor.

1269 Parliament established.

1330s Westminster becomes the home of Parliament.

1381 The Peasants' Revolt, London surrenders to the rebels.

1513 Royal Dockyard at Deptford founded.

1536 Henry VIII orders the dissolution of the monasteries. All London's monasteries are closed in less than ten years.

1540 Lord Mayor's Show begun.

1566 Work begins on the Royal Exchange.

1587 Philip Henslowe opens the Rose theater.

1598 The Globe theater built.

1605 Gunpowder Plot. Guy Fawkes attempts to blow up James I and Parliament.

1631 Work begun on Inigo Jones' church of St. Paul, Convent Garden, completed 1633.

1641 The English Civil War begins. London supports Parliament against the King.

1649 King Charles I executed in Whitehall. The English Civil War ends.

1655 Jews to return to England under the Republic.

1657 First synagogue built in London since the Middle Ages.

1660 Monarchy restored. Charles II enters London.

1665 The Great Plague arrives in London. Thousands of Londoners die.

1666 Great Fire of London. The Medieval City and St. Paul's Cathedral are burnt down.

1675 Sir Christopher Wren starts building work on the new St. Paul's Cathedral, and the Royal Observatory, Greenwich.

1688 Glorious Revolution, James II goes into exile.

1694 Bank of England founded.

1707 & 1709 London Building Acts change the architectural style in London.

1711 St. Paul's Cathedral declared finished by Parliament. Parliament passes the 50 Churches Act.

1737 London Gin Riots.

1738 Work begun on London's second bridge at Westminster, completed 1750.

1747 Lord Lovat executed. This was the last public beheading on Tower Hill.

1750 Horse Guards and the Treasury in Whitehall built, completed 1759.

1759 British Museum opened.

1760 Blackfriars Bridge built, completed 1769.

1773 Stock Exchange opened.

1780 Gordon Riots.

1783 Public executions moved from Tyburn to Newgate Jail.

1801 First Census, London's population is 959,310.

1802 West India Docks opened. The first of many large docks downriver of the Thames.

1811 Vauxhall and Waterloo Bridges begun. Regents Park and Regent's Street development begun by John Nash, including Trafalgar Square and the conversion of Buckingham

House into Buckingham Palace.

1815 Southwark Bridge built.

1820 Regents Canal opened.

1824 London Bridge rebuilt. National Gallery opened.

1825 The first underwater road tunnel in the world constructed under the Thames between Rotherhythe and Wapping (completed 1843).

1826 University College London founded.

1828 King's College founded. St. Katherine's Dock opened.

1829 Metropolitan Police formed. George Shillibeer introduces the first omnibus into London.

1831 Medieval London Bridge replaced.

1834 The Palace of Westminster destroyed by fire. Parliament choses Barry and Pugin to create a new palace in the new Gothic style (completed 1867).

1835 Madam Tussaud's Waxworks opened.

1836 London's first passenger railway opened between Deptford and Bermondsey.

1837 Euston Station opened.

1838 Paddington Station opened.

1839 The City of London Police formed.

1851 The Great Exhibition.

1852 Kings Cross Station opened.

1854 Major cholera epidemic hits London killing 10,738. John Snow proves the link between polluted water and the disease.

1855 Metropolitan Board of Works (M.B.W.) established.

1858 The "Great Stink" from the Thames.

1859 The London General Omnibus Company Ltd. (L.G.O.C.) formed. This will become part of London Transport in 1933.

1863 London's first underground railway line opened by the Metropolitan Railway Company between Paddington Station and Farringdon.

1865 New sewer system installed in London.

1868 Last public executions in London.

1870 The first successful tram routes in London opened. The Royal Albert Hall of Arts and Sciences opened.

1874 Liverpool Street Station opened. Work begins on a new building for the Royal Courts of Justice, in the Strand (completed 1882).

1877 First electric street lights installed in London.

1879 First telephone exchange opens in London.

1880 Royal Albert Dock built.

1886 Shaftesbury Avenue built. Bloody Sunday riot in Trafalgar Square.

1888 London County Council (L.C.C.) formed. Jack the Ripper murders five women in Whitechapel.

1891 Blackwall Tunnel built under the Thames (completed 1897).

1894 Tower Bridge opens.

1897 Harrods built (completed 1905).

1899 The South Kensington Museum of Fine Art and Manufactures split into the Science Museum, and the Victoria and Albert Museum.

1900 Central Criminal Court (Old Bailey) built.

1901 The census records the population of London at 4,536,267.

1903 The Roman Catholic Westminster Cathedral is completed.

1908 Admiralty Arch built on the Mall.

1909 Selfridge's opened.

1914 Last horsedrawn omnibus in London goes out of service. World War I starts.

1915 London bombed from the air for the first time by Zeppelin airships. Germans launch a major bombing offensive against London using airplanes.

1918 World War I ends.

1922 The B.B.C. makes its first radio broadcast from the Strand.

1924 British Empire Exhibition at Wembley.

1933 London Transport created.

1936 First B.B.C. television broadcast from Alexandra Palace, north London.

1939 World War II begins.

1940 The Germans start bombing campaign against London.

1945 Second World War ends. Some 29,890 Londoners were killed in air raids and a further 50,000 badly injured.

1946 Heathrow Airport established as London's airport.

1948 Olympics held in London.

1951 Festival of Britain exhibition.

1952 Trams taken out of service. The "Great Smog" in London is caused by pollution, and responsible for about 5,000 deaths.

1965 London County Council replaced by the Greater London Council (G.L.C.).

1967 East India Dock closes. By 1981 all of London's docks have closed.

1972 Thames flood barrier built in Woolwich.

1981 London Docklands Development Corporation set up to redevelop London's derelict docks.

1986 G.L.C. abolished.

1987 Docklands Light Railway opens. London City Airport opens.

1990s Building of a new financial city at Canary Wharf regenerates eastern London.

2000 Greater London Authority (G.L.A.) established under London's first ever elected mayor. Millennium Dome and London Eye exhibition opened to celebrate the Millennium.

2001 Census finds the population of London to be 7,179,276.

A NOTE ON CURRENCY

Between 1968 and 1973 the United Kingdom introduced decimal currency. The modern British pound (£) is made up of 100 pence, sometimes called new pence. The symbol for a decimal penny is a lower case "p" after the numeral, e.g. £1 = 100p. A colloquial word also used everywhere instead of "pound" is "quid" (the plural is the same). Coins in the United Kingdom are issued in the following denominations:

One Penny	1p
Two Pennies	2p
Five Pence	5p
Ten Pence	10p
Twenty Pence	20p
Fifty Pence	50p
One Pound	£1
Two Pounds	£2
and so on...	

Prior to the introduction of the decimal system, the currency was based on a pound (£) of 20 shillings, and each shilling was worth 12 pennies. There were therefore 240 pennies to the pound. The symbol for an old pre-decimal penny is a lower case 'd' after the numeral, and for a shilling a lower case 's', i.e. £1 = 20s or 240d. This would be written in the form £/s/d or £/s/– in the case of amounts with even shillings; e.g. £5/4s/6d would be five pounds, four shillings and sixpence, £4/7s/– would be four

pounds and seven shillings. Occasionally the 's' and 'd' may be left out, e.g. 4/6 would be four shillings and sixpence. Before decimalization the United Kingdom operated with a bewildering number of different coins. These were the most common:

Farthing	1/4d
Half Penny	1/2d
One Penny	1d
Threepenny bit	3d
Groat	4d
Sixpenny bit	6d
Shilling (s)	1s (12d)
Florin	2s (24d)
Half Crown	2s/6d (30d)
Crown	5s (60d)
Half Sovereign	10s (120d)
Half Guinea	10s/6d
Sovereign	£1 (20s or 240d)
Guinea	£1/1s/–

Below: The Bank of England in the 19th century.

INDEX